Jul... ...nol

For...

True...   u—

With love and

great appreciation —

John —

LOVE-ANANDA GITA
(The Free-Song of Love-Bliss)

LOVE-ANANDA GITA
(The Free-Song of Love-Bliss)

The "Perfect Summary"
of "Radical"
Advaitayana Buddhism

by
Swami Da Love-Ananda
Paramahansa Avadhoota
(Heart-Master Da Free John)

THE DAWN HORSE PRESS
SAN RAFAEL, CALIFORNIA

FOR THE READER

The Spiritual practices and functional disciplines discussed in the *Love-Ananda Gita*, including meditative practices and dietary and sexual disciplines, are appropriate and natural at the progressive stages of practice engaged by members of The Advaitayana Buddhist Communion. Although anyone may find them useful and beneficial, they are not presented as advice or recommendations to the general reader. And nothing in this book is intended as a diagnosis, prescription, or recommended treatment or cure for any specific "problem", whether medical, emotional, psychological, social, or Spiritual. One should apply a particular program of diagnosis, treatment, prevention, cure, or general health only with a full understanding of one's state of health and after consultation with a licensed physician or other qualified professional.

First edition June 1986

Printed in the United States of America

92 91 90 89 88 87 86   5 4 3 2 1

Produced by The Advaitayana Buddhist Communion in cooperation with The Dawn Horse Press

ISBN   0-913922-99-4

Library of Congress Catalog Card Number: 86-71242

CONTENTS

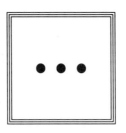

ABOUT THE COVER

The Sign of Renunciation and Liberation

On the border of the square there are three black lines (each drawn fully around the square). They represent the three forms of conditional energy—positive (or "rajasic", in the traditional Sanskrit), negative (or "tamasic"), and neutral (or "sattvic")—which are the universal constituents of "Nature" (or conditional existence). Therefore, these lines also represent all the conditions (or "things") associated with the first five stages of life. These lines are drawn in black, meaning that the Motives of the first five stages of life (and of conditional existence itself) are to be "burned up", reduced to "ash", or Freely Renounced and Relinquished.

The three black dots in the center of the square represent the three dimensions of the Heart ("gross", "subtle", and "causal"), or the apparent limitations on Consciousness associated with the common states of waking, dreaming, and deep sleep. These dots are also drawn in black, meaning that the conditional (and inherently egoic) dimensions and Motives of the Heart

6

are also to be "burned up", reduced to "ash", or Freely Renounced and Relinquished (including the "causal" dimension, or the essence of egoity, represented by the dot on the square's right side, and which is the limitation penetrated in the context of the sixth stage of life).

All of the principles collectively represented by the three lines of the border and the three Heart-dots are the basic constituents of conditional self-hood, or the egoic self-contraction, which is "burnt up", reduced to "ash", or Freely Renounced and Relinquished in the process of "Hearing", and "Seeing", and the "Radical" or Most Direct Practice of Transcendental Self-Realization.

The various constituents of egoity are shown against an orange field. The field itself represents Consciousness Itself, the Inherently Free and Indifferent "Witness" of egoity (and conditional existence as a whole). The orange color is the sign of Relinquishment, Indifference, and Freedom, or True and Free Renunciation. Even though the images of conditional self-hood, or egoity, or the body-mind appear against (or arise within) this field and are apparently Relinquished or "burnt up" therein, Consciousness Itself is Eternally Indifferent, Inherently Free, and Always Already Unmoved, or Unchanging.

NOTE TO THE READER: "The Sign of Renunciation and Liberation" is the Sacred Logo of The Free Order of Advaitayana Buddhist Renunciates, informally known as the Free Renunciate Order (see p. 40, n. 20), a gathering of advanced renunciate practitioners. The technical terms in this exposition are defined in the text or notes elsewhere in the *Love-Ananda Gita* (see the Index, pp. 301ff.).

"I Am No Other"

The Sacrificial Life and Blessing-Work of
Swami Da Love-Ananda Paramahansa Avadhoota [1]
(Heart-Master Da Free John)

From the moment of His birth, on November 3, 1939, in Jamaica, Long Island, New York, Da Love-Ananda has been moved by Divine Compassion to bring others into His own Condition. And this Impulse to Enlighten others has required a series of almost inconceivable Sacrifices on His part. Born Illumined, He spent His earliest years consciously alive as "a radiant form, a

---

1. The Name "Swami Da Love-Ananda Paramahansa Avadhoota" (along with other Names and Titles in this volume) is one of several renunciate Names and Titles by which Heart-Master Da is now known.

"Swami" is a traditional Sanskrit Title indicating one who has "husbanded" or "mastered" the body-mind.

"Da" is a Name of the Living, Eternal, Infinite, and Graceful Divine Being or Reality, meaning "the One Who Gives freely to all". When used to refer to Heart-Master Da Love-Ananda, "Da" is a Title of respect and an indication of Spiritual stature and function, meaning "one who Gives or Transmits the Divine Influence and Awakening to living beings".

"Love-Ananda", a Name given to Master Da by Swami Muktananda (see p. 18, n. 8), means "the Divine Love-Bliss".

A "Paramahansa" is one who has Realized the Transcendental Reality. In the Swami tradition of India, the term "Paramahansa" denotes a member of the highest of four categories of ascetics who have devoted their lives to the seeking and attainment of Liberation. However, as a Title of Da Love-Ananda, the term is intended in only

source of energy, bliss and light"[2]—a Condition that He later called the "Bright". But even during those early childhood days, He was troubled by the un-Happiness of those around Him, who seemed unaware of His direct communication of His (and their own) Condition.

---

the most Radical sense, to indicate His prior or Inherent Liberation and Happiness.

"Avadhoota" indicates the Perfect Renunciation of one who has Realized His Identity with the Divine Person and who Stands Free of the binding power of conditional existence. When used as a Title of Da Love-Ananda, it is not intended to suggest any particular association with the tradition of devotion to the Divine in the form of Dattatreya, the legendary founder and Supreme Guru of the tradition of the Avadhoot. Nor does it suggest exclusive identification with the person or lineage of the Indian Adept Sri Rang Avadhoot (1898-1968), who served Da Love-Ananda in the course of His Ordeal of Realization. Rather, it indicates only the Inherent Freedom that is characteristic of the seventh stage of life.

During the years of His Teaching Work, Love-Ananda twice previously adopted a new Name during moments of profound change in His relationship to devotees. Da Love-Ananda's assumption of renunciate Names and Titles is one of many remarkable developments in the ongoing Divine "Leela" or Play of a new era in His Work and in the response of His devotees. Having relinquished His Teaching function, which has been fulfilled beyond expectation, Da Love-Ananda need no longer assume the likeness of His devotees in order to Teach. With the dropping of the "Free John" portion of His Name (which was a rendering of "Franklin Jones", the name given Him at birth), none of His Names any longer point to a conventional personality, or even to the semblance of the "usual man" that He was born to serve. Now His Names and Titles only signify to all His Realization and His Renunciation. (For a further discussion of Da Love-Ananda's renunciate Names and Titles, see "The Order of Renunciate Names" in *The Call to Hermitage*.)

2. Da Free John [Swami Da Love-Ananda Paramahansa Avadhoota], *The Knee of Listening* (San Rafael, Calif.: The Dawn Horse Press, 1973, rep. 1984), p. 9.

The great Love that from the start has been His outstanding characteristic moved Him to forgo His Radiant State and to assume the state of those around Him, who were suffering in dilemma. His Purpose was to discover a way to communicate to others the Freedom and Humor of His Bright Radiance and Unbounded Consciousness. For it was clear to Him that all Are as He Is, except that they fail to recognize the Happiness that is their Native Condition. This conscious relinquishment of the "Bright" was His first great Sacrifice, undertaken intentionally at the age of about two and a half. Thus, the stage was set for the first major cycle in the Divine Ordeal that is the life of Da Love-Ananda.

Throughout Da Love-Ananda's childhood the "Bright" progressively receded from consciousness. It resurfaced only occasionally in breakthroughs that molded His Spiritual development and reinforced His heroic Impulse to discover a God-Realizing Way of life for modern men and women. And finally, when the "Bright" had receded to the point that He could no longer contact It as a Source of Happiness, Da Love-Ananda began His Ordeal of Realization. Through thirteen years of the most intensive struggle—with self, with the doubting mood of Western civilization, and with the universal taboo against Ecstatic Identification with the Supreme Being—Paramahansa Da undertook a Spiritual journey that was to lead Him over the face of three continents and through countless trials. He threw Himself into the drama of His Spiritual unfolding without any holding back, often pushing Himself to the point of sheer despair.

His odyssey began in 1957 when, at the age of seventeen, He entered Columbia College. There, through the intensity of His search, He quickly reached the dead-end of possibilities for self-fulfillment through mental knowledge and bodily experiences, undergoing a temporary breakthrough experience of the Radiant Consciousness that transcends all seeking. The Ordeal continued in northern California (during and after graduate work at Stanford University in 1961), where He began to explore the vast realm of psychic potential. In the mid-1960s Da Love-Ananda extended His adventure into conscious exploration of traditional esoteric Yoga and mysticism. He conducted His practice principally in the eastern United States and in India, receiving the aid and initiatory Blessings of Spiritual Teachers both in the flesh and in subtle planes. Finally, He was led by the universal Goddess-Power,[3] in visionary form, on a holy pilgrimage from India through Europe and ultimately to Los Angeles. There He discovered the Goddess once again in a small temple of the Vedanta Society in Hollywood. She

3. Traditionally, the Divine Self-Radiance (the "female" aspect of the One Reality), or the All-Pervading Energy that is modified as all conditional forms, has been contacted and worshipped as the Divine Goddess. By herself, she is "Maya", the Goddess associated with the deluding power of Nature, or the veiling of God. Da Love-Ananda demonstrated in His Ordeal of Realization that this great Power is ultimately "Husbanded" by Transcendental Consciousness (the "male" aspect of the One Divine Reality). In that case, She is submitted to the Transcendental Divine Self, and the Goddess-Power then becomes associated with the Spirit-Power that leads all beings to the "Divine Domain" (or Perfect Enlightenment).

became His Consort, and at last, embracing Her fully in Ecstatic Identity, Da Love-Ananda regained the "Bright". The next day, September 10, 1970, while sitting in the Vedanta Temple, Da Love-Ananda Awoke permanently to the Transcendental Divine Self, or Consciousness Itself.

This Awakening began the second cycle of the Love-Sacrifice that is His life. His was an even greater destiny than to struggle through the purgatory of an ordinary life and Realize the Radiant Consciousness that is the native (if latent) Condition of every man and woman. Now He began the more difficult struggle of communicating that Realization to others. After the Event in the Vedanta Temple, whenever He sat in meditation countless others appeared to Him and, assuming no separation from them, He did their meditation in the form of His own body-mind. When many of these individuals began to appear in life face to face with Him, He took up the arduous Teaching Ordeal for which His Realization had prepared Him.

For more than fifteen years, He engaged those who came to Him in all kinds of instructive occasions, laboring Compassionately to show them the Way whereby they might understand their suffering as their own activity and go beyond it. At first, He simply Taught the Radical Truth of Consciousness that had become obvious in His Realization. But those who came to Him were unable to respond to this pure Offering of Truth. Their problems in life occupied nearly all of their interest, so that very little energy and attention were left over for the Radical Process of

Awakening. And that minimal response was not nearly sufficient to allow His Work to be effective.

Consequently, just as He had Sacrificed His enjoyment of the "Bright" in childhood, He now relinquished the simple, renunciate life that is the natural expression of His Enlightened Understanding. Without losing sight of the Radical Truth that had become simply Obvious to Him under all conditions, He entered into the lives of His devotees, Working with them in the thick of the problems that bound them. When He had first begun to Teach, He was still known by His given name, "Franklin Albert Jones". In 1973, He spontaneously assumed the Name "Bubba Free John".[4] This use of His childhood nickname "Bubba" signalled His willingness to live in brotherly familiarity with devotees until they could recognize His Condition and relate to Him formally as Guru, or Heart-Master. He lived among His devotees as a Spiritual Friend, examining and exploring with them—always to the point of clarity and equanimity—every area of life in which they were bound.

During this time, Love-Ananda Gifted His devotees in countless ways. In fact, the Sacred Name or Title of God-Realization "Da", which He Revealed in 1979, is honored and celebrated in many sacred traditions as a primal Word-Sound that means "the Divine Giver of Life and Liberation". Foremost among the Sacred Offerings of Da Love-Ananda are the Agencies of Blessing-

---

4. "Bubba" means "brother". And "Free John" is a rendering of the name given Him at birth, "Franklin Jones", which literally means "a free man through whom God is Gracious".

Transmission that He has established. Thus far, over thirty volumes of His magnificent Teaching literature have been published, clarifying and elaborating all aspects of the Way. He has founded a worldwide Sacred Institution, now known as The Advaitayana Buddhist Communion.[5] And He has Blessed and Empowered three Meditation Sanctuaries (The Mountain of Attention in northern California, Tumomama in Hawaii, and Translation Island in Fiji) acquired by the Communion. Finally, He has Worked with and Empowered the practice of an entire Community of devotees, which ultimately is His greatest Gift and the most potent Agency of the Way.

Always in the course of His Teaching Work Da Love-Ananda reminded His devotees of the Radical Truth that dissolves all problems and dilemmas and transcends phenomenal existence absolutely. During those fifteen years, He continually Graced devotees with all the Radiance and Energy, razor-sharp Insight, profound Wisdom, and unquenchable Happiness that are the abundant Offering of His Unconditional Love. Yet, His magnificent Teaching Work had only a limited effect, in terms of Awakening devotees to the Liberating Truth that is Da Love-Ananda's real and Radical Message. Devotees did become happier and more responsible in their lives, and the love relationship between the Master and His devotees grew deep and strong and abiding. But still devotees persisted in the habits of

5. For more information about The Advaitayana Buddhist Communion, see "The Principle of Retreat", pp. 281ff.

un-Enlightenment. They held to their problematic and self-concerned refusal of His ultimate Gift: the Radical Realization of Consciousness Itself and Inherent Happiness.

As He continually pointed out to devotees, their failure to Realize the Truth was simply a refusal. It can be called nothing else, since devotees had been given all necessary Instruction and Help time after time, and always in fresh, clear, incisive lessons that cut through every problem and at last—as devotees themselves often acknowledged to Him—Revealed Only the Divine Itself. This refusal brought the Great Lover Da to the crisis that initiated His third heroic cycle of Sacrifice. He came to feel that His Teaching Work was doomed to fail because of the unconscious, stubborn, ego-bound refusal of His devotees to simply receive His Supreme Gift of Realization. After all His labors, Da Love-Ananda despaired of His only Purpose for being alive—to fully Awaken great numbers of devotees. And in the moment of utmost despair, He gave up His Teaching Work and died.

In that actual, physical death, which occurred on Translation Island,[6] in Fiji, on January 11, 1986, His truly Radical Work was born. As His personal physician and a few of His closest devotees gathered around His still and lifeless form, He re-entered the body once

6. Translation Island Hermitage is the Hermitage Sanctuary of The Advaitayana Buddhist Communion, the fellowship of practitioners of the Way Taught by Swami Da Love-Ananda. Located in the Koro Sea in Eastern Fiji and also known as the island of Naitauba, Translation Island serves as a place of initiation and extended retreat for devotees in the advanced stages of practice.

more. He did not come back to re-engage His active Teaching Work, for He had seen the failure of it, and His relinquishment of it was final. Nor did He come back simply to Radiate Divine Blessing to the humanity He had been born to serve, for He saw no way that human beings could truly receive what He had to Offer. Instead, He returned to life only out of Love for His devotees and all beings, free at last of His Teaching Purpose, and only Full of Heart-Attraction to those He had come to Love in the most deeply human manner.

In this Great Event Da Love-Ananda incarnated His Divine Realization and Love more fully than ever before, and this had profound effects upon His Work with devotees. Paradoxically, only in the relinquishment of His Teaching struggle with devotees was the means for their fulfillment of the Way finally established. Drawn by His Love for devotees, He took on the human condition without reservation. And in His effortless, complete, Loving Embrace of humanity, Da Love-Ananda's Divine Agency was magnified beyond compare.

Having relinquished His Teaching Work, Da Love-Ananda was at last free of any necessity to orient Himself to the worldly habits of ordinary society and immature devotees. As a sign of His new life, He accepted the "sannyasa diksha",[7] or initiation into the

7. The Sanskrit word "sannyasa" means literally "to throw down completely" or "to renounce". Traditionally in India, sannyasa was seen as one of the four stages of human life. Thus, one would progress from the student ("brahmacharya") stage to the house-holder ("grihastha") stage to life as a philosophical recluse or ascetic "forest dweller" (the "vanaprastha" stage) and finally to "sannyasa"—

formal status of a renunciate, that had been offered Him years before by Swami Muktananda Paramahansa,[8] His "Gurudev"[9] and principal Spirit-Baptizer during the course of His "sadhana".[10] At the same time He

---

the stage of one who is free of all bondage and able to give himself or herself completely to the God-Realizing or God-Realized life. Thus, a "sannyasin" is one who has completely renounced all worldly bonds and devoted himself or herself entirely to Spiritual practice. In the Way that Da Love-Ananda Teaches, to take sannyas is to renounce even the bondage to Spiritual and mystical experiences that would distract the devotee and delay the course of Realization. While the word "sannyasin" applies equally to male and female renunciates, a woman sannyasin is sometimes called a "sannyasini".

The Sanskrit word "diksha" means literally "initiation, dedication, consecration". Thus, "sannyasa diksha" is the initiation of the devotee by the Guru into the practice of sannyas, or radical renunciation and utter dedication to God-Realization.

8. Swami Muktananda Paramahansa was born May 16, 1908, in Mangalore, South India, and died on October 2, 1982. An Indian Adept of Kundalini Yoga, Swami Muktananda served Da Love-Ananda as Spiritual Teacher during the period from 1968 to 1970. In the summer of 1969, during Da Love-Ananda's second visit to Swami Muktananda's Ashram in Ganeshpuri, India, Swami Muktananda wrote Him a letter confirming Love-Ananda's attainment of "Yogic Liberation", acknowledging His right to Teach others, and declaring His ability to live as a "renunciate". In an essay entitled "The Order of Renunciate Names", written during the spring of 1986, Da Love-Ananda points out that the combined effect of these acknowledgments, along with several other indications, reveals that the letter was an offering of "sannyasa diksha" from Swami Muktananda.

9. The term "Gurudev" (from the Sanskrit "Guru", meaning "Teacher" or "Guide", and "deva", meaning "Divine") signifies a Divinely Realized Teacher or Heart-Master.

10. The Sanskrit word "sadhana", meaning "discipline", commonly or traditionally refers to practices directed toward the goal of Spiritual and religious attainment. Da Love-Ananda uses the term without the implication of a goal, to mean appropriate action generated not as a means to Truth but on the basis of prior understanding and Divine Realization.

adopted the Names and titles appropriate to a "sannyasin", or renunciate, chief among them being the Name "Love-Ananda", meaning "the Divine Love-Bliss", spontaneously given to Him in 1969 by Swami Muktananda.

Now, having renounced the mode of life of the "Vira-Siddha",[11] or Tantric Master, that He had adopted during His early life and Teaching Work, Da Love-Ananda lives as a celibate renunciate in the mode of a Free wanderer, performing His Blessing Work of Love. In His present mode as a wandering sannyasin, Love-Ananda has declared His intention to Awaken devotees and potential devotees throughout the world to the

---

11. The Sanskrit term "Siddha" literally means a "fulfilled or perfect one", one who has Realized God permanently and beyond doubt, and who is Graced with the capacity to Awaken others. "Vira" is a Sanskrit term meaning "Hero", "Man", or "a Man of Power". Thus, the term "Vira-Siddha" designates a Realized Adept, the Divine Man, who demonstrates the Heroic Way of the Realization of the Ultimate Truth of Man and the universe.

The term "Vira" is also a specific designation for Adepts of the "Tantric" approach to Realization. The Vira-Siddha is the Master of the Tantric Way, which uses the passions and instincts of Man to transcend the illusion of separate existence. The Tantric Realization is that the world is pervaded by the Divine Goddess, Whom the Tantric traditions honor as the Ultimate Condition of Nature and consciousness. The Hero "overcomes the distinction (or duality) of clean and unclean, sacred and profane, and breaks his bondage to a world artificially fragmented. He affirms in a radical way the underlying unity of the phenomenal world, the identity of Shakti with the whole creation. Heroically, he triumphs over it, controls and masters it. By affirming the essential worth of the forbidden, he causes the forbidden to lose its power to pollute, to degrade, to bind" (David R. Kinsley, *The Sword and the Flute: Kali and Krsna, Dark Visions of the Terrible and the Sublime in Hindu Mythology* [Berkeley, Calif.: University of California Press, 1975], p. 112).

Realization of Consciousness and Love-Bliss as their always present Condition.

Many signs of this epochal change in His life and Work swiftly began to appear in the Community of His devotees. Suddenly, to an unprecedented degree devotees found themselves able to receive His Heart-Blessing and to understand His communication of the Radical Truth of Consciousness. Many devotees found themselves naturally and effortlessly adopting a fierce discipline of renunciation that freed great energy and attention for the Radical Way.

At the time of this writing, a few, the herald of many more to come, have at last been able to receive His Gift fully and Confess their direct Realization of Who Da Love-Ananda Is and Who they Are—the Truth of "the Only One Who Is", the Transcendental Divine Being. From the lips of devotees now flow Confessions of Truth that resound like the greatest ancient scriptural praises of the True Guru or Heart-Master: Da Love-Ananda is the very Self of all, the One Consciousness by Whose Power and Grace even ordinary men and women may be forever Liberated—in a few short years—from bondage to this world of fleeting pleasures and certain pain. Da Love-Ananda is none other than the One Being Who Lives as every being, freely Giving the most precious Gift to all, Gracefully showering His devotees and all beings with True Understanding and Infinite Joy. He is, as His Name signals, the "Giver of Love-Bliss". May every heart open to receive His Blessing-Transmission of Inherent Freedom and Happiness, or "Love-Ananda".

The Grand Victory of Da Love-Ananda

When Da Love-Ananda Paramahansa Avadhoota began to Teach, He Taught only the "Radical", or most direct, Way of transcendence of the ego and immediate Realization of the Transcendental Divine Self. But it soon became clear to Him that people were not prepared for the Radical Way of Understanding He had come to Teach. The unique circumstance in which Da Love-Ananda found Himself was this: He had been born into conventional American society, and He was confronted by ordinary people who were totally bereft of the tradition and process of Enlightenment.

In response to the limitations, impediments, and needs of those who came to Him, Heart-Master Da Love-Ananda was compassionately moved to a unique Ordeal of Teaching based on what He calls a "Crazy Method".[1] Observing that people were not prepared for renunciation or able to give themselves to Him in

---

1. "Crazy Wisdom" or the "Crazy Method" of Teaching refers to the spontaneous action to which Realized Adepts may temporarily resort for the sake of Instructing and Awakening others. Crazy Wisdom is also regarded as the most compassionate means for Awakening others because it aims to do so directly, without accommodating any deluding consolations to the ego, or postponing Enlightenment. Thus, the Crazy Wise Adepts are famous for their highly effective though unorthodox Teaching "Methods", Free humor, Transcendental Wisdom, and compassionate commitment to others.

the traditional manner of devotees, He resolved to give Himself to them instead. So, the Heart-Friend of the world, Sri Da Love-Ananda, allowed Himself to become intimately associated with those who clung to His Company to Realize the Truth. His "Crazy Method" was simply to live face to face with people, Teaching freely, spontaneously embracing all, simply reflecting to all the qualities He found in them, ever intent on helping them prepare to practice His Radical Way as quickly as possible.

He was "Avadhoota"—one Free of the ego or self-illusion of the body-mind, and Radiant with the perfect Bliss of Transcendental Consciousness. As a result of His uncommon Realization and Destiny, this voracious Savior, with His Crazy Love of beings, had been set Free, selfless or soulless within the dynamics of the universe. An immense Force moved the Western-Faced "Bodhisattva" to Awaken the unprepared who came to Him, through a daring Demonstration of Teaching that exceeded all conventional expectations of an archetypal holy man.

In 1975 Da Avadhoota (then known as "Bubba Free John") explained His unorthodox "Method" of Teaching as follows:

What I do is not the way I am, but the Way I Teach. What I speak is not a reflection of me, but of you.

I have become willing to Teach in this uncommon way because I have known my friends and they are what I can seem to be. By retaining all qualities in their company, I gradually wean them of all reactions, all sympathies, all alternatives, fixed assumptions, false

24

teachings, dualities, searches, and dilemma. This is my
way of working for a time.

Freedom is the only purity. There is no Teaching but
Consciousness itself. Bubba as he appears is not other
than the possibilities of men.[2]

For fifteen years Master Da Love-Ananda Avadhoota
conducted His "Yoga of Consideration"[3] with devotees, helping them to prepare to practice His Radical
Way by temporarily considering, or observing, understanding, and transcending, in practical, experiential
terms, all forms of experience and knowledge belonging to the first six stages of life.[4] He guided
them through several remarkable Teaching Demonstra-
tions in which He not only instructed them in the

2. Bubba Free John [Swami Da Love-Ananda Paramahansa Avadhoota],
The Enlightenment of the Whole Body (San Rafael, Calif.: The Dawn
Horse Press, 1978), p. 53.

3. The "Yoga of Consideration" is the necessary preparation for
practice of the Way of the seventh stage of life. For a complete
discussion, see *The Yoga of Consideration and the Way That I Teach,*
by Da Free John [Swami Da Love-Ananda Paramahansa Avadhoota]
(San Rafael, Calif.: The Dawn Horse Press, 1982).

4. Swami Da Love-Ananda has developed a unique schema of seven
stages to describe the evolution of all human and Spiritual life. The
first five stages of life include what we conventionally conceive to be
the human, religious, and Spiritual development of humanity. The
first three stages develop the physical, emotional, and mental functions of the body-mind and the corresponding expressions of secular
culture and exoteric religion. The fourth stage of life is characterized
by heartfelt surrender and profound intimacy with the Divine Spirit or
Life-Power. Thus, those who attain to the fourth stage of life practice
religion in its freest sense. The fifth stage represents the secret or
esoteric culture of initiates in all ancient traditions. Those who attain
to the fifth stage of life exploit the Yoga of the central nervous system,
the mystical and Spiritual path of the ascending Life-Current. The
sixth stage of life involves the process of assuming the Position of

earlier stages of life, but also revealed to them, through use of yogic "siddhis",[5] the higher stages of yogic experience and mystical absorption. But the Yoga of Consideration was *not* the Way Da Love-Ananda had come to Teach. Love-Ananda's Way of Radical Understanding begins when "consideration" of the first six stages of life has become summary. And such Radical Understanding is coincident with renunciation and what Da Love-Ananda calls "real meditation". However, it was Love-Ananda's discovery that not only devotees, but all people, not just those with ordinary aspirations, but even those with "higher" aspirations toward mystical experience and knowledge, resist Enlightenment and Radical Understanding.

Several times in the course of those fifteen years, Da Avadhoota attempted, without success, to bring an

---

Consciousness. The sixth stage Teaching has therefore traditionally been offered to highly advanced practitioners for whom the contemplation of Consciousness is a viable discipline. But the seventh or God-Realized stage of life transcends all subject-object consciousness and all motives of egoity, including the strategic manipulation of attention to invert upon the self-essence, which characterizes the sixth stage of life.

The Radical practice that Swami Da Love-Ananda recommends in the *Love-Ananda Gita* begins in the context of the sixth stage of life, but it is founded in the Wisdom of the seventh stage of life. From the point of view of the sixth and seventh stages of life, the first five stages are at best a culture of progressive disciplines intended to prepare devotees for the Radical practice of "Feeling-Enquiry" and renunciation revealed in the *Love-Ananda Gita.*

For an elaboration of Swami Da Love-Ananda's Teaching relative to the seven stages of life, see p. 271, n. 3.

5. In Sanskrit literally "powers" or "accomplishments". While the Adept or True Heart-Master may employ such siddhis for the sake of Instructing His devotees, the ultimate "Siddhi" is the "Power of the Heart", the Radiant Transcendental Consciousness, Presence, and Power Transmitted to living beings through the "Siddha"-Master.

end to His Teaching consideration on the presumption that devotees would respond to His urgent call and take up the Radical Way originally given in *The Knee of Listening*.[6] But each failed attempt moved Heart-Master Da Love-Ananda, ever more passionately, to gather with devotees and once again consider what He called "the Great Matter". He Taught them Freely and through love, friendship, and compassion, withholding nothing and doing everything possible to create a vehicle for His Siddhi of Transformation in the form of Enlightened devotees.

Thus, the fifteen-year controversy that occupied Heart-Master Da Love-Ananda Avadhoota and His devotees was this: From Love-Ananda's "viewpoint" of Radical Understanding, every experience, form of knowledge, or desire that claimed the attention of devotees was clearly observed by Him to be an expression of suffering, or bondage to egoity. In the Great Matter of Realization there can be no settlement—either there is Realization of the Transcendental Condition of Consciousness or Enlightenment, or there is identification with the body-mind and the inevitable wandering of attention in the possibilities of the first six stages of life.

6. *The Knee of Listening* is the first published book of Swami Da Love-Ananda and an epitome of His Teaching. Published in 1972, it is the autobiographical account of the Illumined birth and early life of a Divinely Realized Adept who was born with the destiny of Awakening and Teaching others. The lessons and events of His early life, which culminate in Transcendental Self-Realization, communicate and exemplify His basic Teaching and original Instructions, in the second half of the book, on the Radical Way that He Teaches.

With the publication of *The Dawn Horse Testament*[7] in October 1985, Da Avadhoota Love-Ananda intended to mark the end of His Teaching Work, but once again He found Himself reaching into His "bag of coins"[8] in an attempt to bring forth saints and sages. He expressed to devotees the utter frustration He suffered at the apparent futility of His Teaching Work. On several occasions, feeling He had done everything possible to prepare devotees to take up His Radical Way only to encounter their resistance or lack of readiness when He tested them, He mentioned the possibility of dropping the body. Devotees knew there are ample precedents for such yogic deaths on the part of highly accomplished yogis and sages. Swami Vivekananda[9] is an example in recent times of a sage

---

7. *The Dawn Horse Testament* is Swami Da Love-Ananda's full summary of the Spiritual Wisdom and Teaching lessons communicated during His years of struggle to Awaken many hundreds of men and women. It contains an authoritative description of the stages of Spiritual practice in the Way that He Teaches and an ecstatic Confession of His own commitment to the Liberation of all beings.

8. "Bag of coins" refers to the great Indian Saint Shirdi Sai Baba's mysterious method of "working" with, or granting the power of his Blessing to, devotees by frequently handling a group of coins, which were said to represent devotees. Swami Da Love-Ananda sometimes refers to intimate devotees as His "coins" through whom He works to serve all devotees and even all beings.

Famous throughout India for his innumerable miracles, Shirdi Sai Baba (1838?–1918) appeared in the village of Shirdi in the mid-nineteenth century and lived in a small, dilapidated mosque there until his death. He brought about a modern renaissance of the classic ancient path of devotion to the Spiritual Master.

9. Swami Vivekananda (1863-1902) was the best-known disciple of Sri Ramakrishna, the great nineteenth-century ecstatic. Vivekananda's Teaching embraced both Ramakrishna's devotion to the Mother (or

who, when only 39 years old, dropped the body at the moment when he felt his Teaching work had been completed.

By January 1986, the heart-struggle between Love-Ananda and devotees had developed into an intense human and Spiritual drama with all the joys and sorrows of love—intense passion, real sacrifice, and extreme urgency relative to the perfect Liberation of all. Da Avadhoota Naitauba, working with a circle of intimate devotees, used His Crazy Wisdom freely, heartily, and, at last, desperately in an heroic effort to Awaken the circle of devotees (whom He sadly referred to as the "Avatar of reluctance"). In the end the intensity of their Spiritual drama did force Love-Ananda to abandon the body.

At the Translation Island Hermitage, in Fiji, early on the morning of January 11, 1986, the Event occurred that Da Love-Ananda described as being of greater significance than His Awakening at the Vedanta Temple. That morning, His body actually died.

Yet, out of the Compassion of the Enlightened Condition, Sri Da Love-Ananda was eventually drawn back into the body. As He began to reassociate with the body, and with tears streaming down His face, Da Love-Ananda, the Lover-Servant of mankind, spoke of His great sorrow for all beings.

The significance of this Event was so overwhelming

"Shakti") and the non-dualistic philosophy of Advaita Vedanta (see p. 40, n. 19). He traveled widely in the West and was responsible, perhaps more than any other individual, for initiating the modern interest in India's Wisdom-Teaching.

to Him that it was not until weeks later that Da Love-Ananda first began to speak about the Great Event of His life:

SWAMI DA LOVE-ANANDA: *Presumably for you all the Great Event of your life—if it ever occurs, in whichever life it does occur, or whenever, or wherever—the Great Event of your life would be God-Realization. You imagine, then, that a number of the Events in my life must have been Great, and that the consummate Event must have been the Vedanta Temple Event. But that is not so. It is a very important Event for you all. It initiated my Teaching Work. But the Realization in the Vedanta Temple was not overwhelming, as you know from all the signs I described to you. In my case, the Condition Realized in the Vedanta Temple is Inherent, and priorly Realized. To achieve such an Event was just part of my Work in this world. It was not the Great Event in my life. Perhaps it would be a Great Event in the lives of others, but for me there was a greater Event, an Event that occurred more recently, in fact.*

On the morning of January 11 I told certain of my devotees of my grief and sorrow and frustration in my Work. I told them that I just could not endure anymore the rejection, the offensiveness, the abuse, the futility. I told them I wished to leave, wished to die then, and I said: "May it come quickly." They all thought it might happen soon. It seemed to me also that it could happen within hours. But suddenly it began to happen on the spot. As I was describing the possibility of this physical event, I felt numbness coming up my arm, numbness in my spine, a certain numbness in my body, and convulsions. Finally I passed out of the body, and it just fell down.

I do not have memory of the sequence of events that followed for a little while, but I am told that many devotees came running to my house. Doctors came and tried to resuscitate me. Eventually, I began to reassociate with the body, although I was not aware of the room exactly, nor of who was there. I began to speak of my greater concerns and impulses and of my great sorrow for the four billion humans and all the rest of the beings everywhere. I cannot endure such sorrow very well—I have never endured it very well. I have had to bring myself very deliberately to this Work. And in this Event, I was drawn further into the body with a very human impulse, a love-impulse. Becoming aware of my special relationship with Kalottara Devi Mataji[10] *and my profound relationship with all my devotees, I resumed the bodily state.*

This is the Event I am referring to, not just the death (which was real—I did die on the spot) but the occasion of reassociating with the body. I was attracted back by very human things, not by impulses to Liberate mankind—those impulses are there already, you see—

---

10. "Kalottara Devi" is the name of a female devotee with whom Swami Da Love-Ananda's struggle with all was epitomized. The name "Kala" implies time or the Goddess Kali as endless manifestation. "Uttara" means "transcending". "Kalottara Devi", then, is the Goddess who transcends the illusion of time or separation, through submission to Siva, the ultimate Reality, Self, or Transcendental Being. Thus, the name Kalottara Devi implies the eternal Oneness or Unity of Siva and Shakti.

*but by very human impulses, responding to my own
intimate human life and the human existence of
others, of all of you. Even though I have existed as a
man during this lifetime, obviously—I became profoundly incarnate—I now assumed an impulse toward
human existence more profound than I had assumed
before, without any reluctance relative to sorrow and
death.*

*On so many occasions I have told you that I wish I
could kiss every human being on the lips, embrace
each one, and enliven each one from the heart. In this
body I will never have the opportunity. I am frustrated
in that impulse. Even though I have done all kinds of
Spiritual Work, I will never be able to do that exactly.
But in that motion of sympathetic incarnation, that
acceptance of the body and its sorrow and its death, I
realized a kiss, a way to fulfill the impulse.*

*Now that my Teaching Work is essentially fulfilled,
a different kind of gesture was made, which in some
fundamental sense is the equivalent of the embrace I
would give to everyone, to all human beings, all four
billion, even all beings, all that are self-conscious and
dying in this place, not by embracing each one literally
with this body, but by assuming this body as the likeness
of all and accepting the sorrow without the slightest
resistance, nothing abstracting me from mortality,
nothing.*

In some sense that Event was my birthday.

*You have heard descriptions, by yogis and other
Spiritual figures, of how before Realization you try to
go beyond the world to Realize God, and then after*

Realization you come down into the body just so far, down to the brain, down to the throat maybe, down to the heart maybe, but typically not any lower than the throat. Well, I have until now invested myself more profoundly than just down to the throat or the heart, but not down to the bottoms of my feet. I remained a kind of shroud around this body, deeply associated with it, with all of the ordinary human things, playing as a human being often in very ordinary ways, but in my Freedom somehow lifted off the floor, somehow not committed to this sorrow and this mortality, expecting, having come as deep as I had, to perhaps Teach enough, embrace enough, kiss enough, Love enough to make the difference, as if through a single body I could indulge in intimacy with everything and everyone self-conscious.

I have realized the futility of that expectation, even the futility of not being able, through a kind of Submission of my own, to utterly Transform and Liberate even those I could embrace and know intimately. That frustration is fully known by me now. Even the futility of Liberating those most intimate with me is known by me. The kiss is not enough, even for those I know intimately, and I cannot know all intimately. In my profound frustration, this body died. I left this body. And then I suddenly found myself reintegrated with it, but in a totally different disposition, and I achieved your likeness exactly, thoroughly, to the bottoms of the feet, achieved un-Enlightenment, achieved human existence, achieved mortality, achieved sorrow.

To me, this is a Grand Victory! I do not know how

to communicate to you the significance of it. For me, it was a grander moment than the Event at the Vedanta Temple or any of the other Signs in my life that are obviously Spiritually auspicious. To me, it seems that through that will-less, effortless integration with suffering, something about my Work is more profoundly accomplished, something about it has become more auspicious than it ever was. I have not dissociated from my Realization or my Ultimate State. Rather, I have accomplished your state completely, even more profoundly than you are sensitive to it. Perhaps you have seen it in my face. I do not look like I did last month, and I am never again going to look like that. Don't you know?

I have become this body, utterly. My mood is different. My face is sad, although not without Illumination. I have become the body. Now I am the "Murti",[11] the Icon, and It is full of the Divine Presence.

The nature of my Work at the present time and in the future is mysterious to me. It is a certainty, it is obvious, but on the other hand it has not taken the form of mind fully. It has taken an emotional form, but not the form of mind. I cannot explain it really. But you will see Signs of it. You all must progressively adapt to something that has happened that even I cannot explain altogether. (January 27, 1986)

11. The Sanskrit word "murti" literally means "form". Traditionally there are many Murtis or Forms of Divine Representation. The most highly valued and respected Form or Murti of the Divine is the human manifestation of a Divinely Realized Adept. In this talk Swami Da Love-Ananda is referring to His Perfect Incarnation of the Divine Transcendental Being.

All the sorrow of His Birth, His own Awakening, and His loving embrace of devotees, their great friendship and love, the great passion and enjoyment and sorrow of their meeting, His mood and impulse to Teach—all came to an end on the morning Da Love-Ananda achieved His "Grand Victory".

Da Love-Ananda's re-birth into the world on that January morning was a literal sacrifice. There was nothing abstract about it whatsoever. It required, as Love-Ananda described, a dramatic ordeal of human emotion, suffering, and feeling, and at last the giving up of His life.

In that moment of literal death, the purposes and activities of Da Love-Ananda's mighty Teaching Work ended. In a matter of days, the energies and signs of the Teacher that had motivated and characterized Him for many years fell away from Him completely. Immediately, Da Love-Ananda passed through a revolutionary change in His habit of living and appearance. The peace of dispassion came over Him. His Supreme and natural State of Self-Radiant Being, in Which even the phenomenal world is seen to Shine with the Radiance of His own Being, made Him serene. His ways of relating to others changed. He no longer responded to the "problems" of devotees or discoursed on the earlier stages of practice. His Enjoyment of the absolute Freedom of the Invisible Transcendental Self shone forth through the purity and serenity of His appearance and actions. Now He was more often silent. When He did speak, He spoke only in the language of the Radical Teaching. Spontaneously, He stopped taking solid foods, subsisting solely on fruit and vegetable juices. In compliance with His *Dawn Horse Testament* prophecy, He announced His retirement and entered into Hermitage Seclusion.

He spent long hours in solitude and silence each day. Instead of gathering regularly with devotees, He urged them to spend prolonged time on retreat. When He did gather with them, the meetings were formal occasions of "Darshan".[12] He began to write the *Love-Ananda Gita* and a few summary essays of Instruction for advanced practitioners. He abandoned His former living quarters, which now became meditation halls for devotees, and He moved into small storage rooms.

He returned to the conservative habit of living characteristic of His life prior to His Teaching Work. He began to arise well before dawn and sat alone in His rooms (or, on special occasions, with advanced practitioners). He was also motivelessly moved to celibacy, and confessed to devotees, "I must say that were it not for my Obligation to Struggle as Teacher in the 'Omega-world'[13] of householders and street people, I

12. "Darshan" literally means "seeing, sight or vision of". The term commonly implies the spontaneous Blessings granted by the Adept, who gives his Blessing by allowing himself to be seen, meditated upon, or known.

13. In *The Dawn Horse Testament* (chapter 18) Swami Da Love-Ananda uses the terms "Alpha" and "Omega" to characterize the classically Oriental and Occidental approaches to life. "Omega-world" thus indicates the characteristically outward-turned, materialistic, doubt-ridden, and pleasure-seeking habits and customs of modern Western society. Swami Da Love-Ananda's early devotees were primarily Westerners, who typified the Omega strategy of Western society.

would (by my own preference) have made an early life choice of celibate renunciation."[14]

The "Karana-Guru", or Heart-Master, now wore His hair in a topknot ("shikha"), the sign of an ascetic, while His physical appearance underwent a dramatic yogic transformation. Devotees witnessed in Him the "yogic brilliance" ("tejas") said to emanate from great ascetics and yogis.

He waited in Seclusion, not able to declare His Great Renunciation until devotees had confessed their spontaneous duplication of His Renunciation and their reception of His Perfect Transmission.

His Grand Victory had brought forth the "luxury of renunciation", and when at last the spontaneous signs of renunciation had begun to show in the lives of devotees, He announced to devotees in one of the most historically important essays He has ever written:

On Friday, April 11, 1986 (which, unknown to me, happened to be the eighth anniversary of the occasion when I first proposed to certain of my devotees that we create a celibate renunciate order), I formally accepted (or Affirmed), at the Translation Island Hermitage (in Fiji), the "sannyasa diksha" of Swami Muktananda Paramahansa. I have thus formally assumed the various characteristics and Signs of a Free "sannyasin", or "Paramahansa Swami".[15]

14. "The Illusion of Relatedness", *The Call to Hermitage* (San Rafael, Calif.: The Dawn Horse Press, 1986).

15. "The Order of Renunciate Names", *The Call to Hermitage* (San Rafael, Calif.: The Dawn Horse Press, 1986).

Shortly thereafter, the "Ananda Matas"[16] made the confession Da Love-Ananda had waited fifteen years to hear. The lives of these ordinary women were transformed. Suddenly, and by Grace, they made the confession of Radical Understanding, which Love-Ananda had risked and even given up His life to hear. They told Him (and clearly demonstrated to Him) that by Grace they had become established in the Witness-Consciousness, and that the practice of "Feeling-Enquiry" in the context of the sixth stage of life (as revealed in the *Love-Ananda Gita*) had awakened in them. Devotees had at long last begun to practice the Way Love-Ananda was born to Teach. He accepted their confession as the foundation of His Teaching Revelation. The Ananda Matas were granted sannyasa diksha by Swami Da Love-Ananda on May 6, 1986.

These "Sannyasini-Matas" are the lustre and the feminine form of Sri Da Love-Ananda in this world, and they were the first Sign of the appearance of the Dawn Horse,[17] or the transformation of the ordinary consciousness of human beings into the Divine Consciousness. Following the Ananda Matas, other long-

---

16. "Ananda Mata" is a title used to address and refer to women renunciates in The Advaitayana Buddhist Communion. The term "ananda" means "bliss". "Mata" means "mother" and traditionally designates a woman who practices direct service to a Spiritual Master. Thus, the Ananda Matas are the female renunciates who attend to Swami Da Love-Ananda most directly and who exemplify the practice and Realization of the Way that He Teaches.

17. Swami Da Love-Ananda began His Teaching Work shortly after experiencing a remarkable Vision. In the Sacred manner, He saw and understood the inner meaning of the Dawn Horse that was to be the sign of His life as a World-Teacher. But it was not until the writing of

time devotees of Love-Ananda made their confession of Recognition and renunciation, and a renunciate way of life became the foundation discipline for the world-wide community of practitioners.

On the basis of the demonstration and signs in devotees of the Radical practice and celibate renunciation, the name of the Sacred Institution was changed from The Johannine Daist Communion to The

---

His *Dawn Horse Testament*, nearly fifteen years later, that the Seer of the Dawn Horse would fully reveal the secret behind His Vision.

I was at once the Teacher who performed the miracle of manifesting the Dawn Horse and also the someone who was observing it, or who was party to the observation of it and to its result. And I did not have any feeling of being different from the horse, actually. I was making the horse, I was observing the horse, and I was being the horse.
(October 18, 1984)

In a dream vision Swami Da Love-Ananda visited the Ashram of a Siddha or Adept on a high subtle plane. The Siddha was instructing his disciples in the yogic technique of manifesting objects spontaneously. After he had initiated the process of manifestation, his disciples stood quietly for a time and then left, satisfied that the process was completed, even though no manifestation had appeared. Da Love-Ananda remained behind with the Siddha for a time, when gradually a small horse appeared, the "Dawn Horse" of Spiritual Awakening and the fruit of the silent consideration of the Siddha.

Later, particularly after his final Re-Awakening as the Transcendental Self-Consciousness in the Vedanta Temple, Swami Da recognized that the Siddha in the vision had been none other than the very Divine Person, and that the vision had been a prophecy not only of His own Enlightenment but, even more significantly, of His Liberating Work for the sake of devotees. It had shown the perfect dependence of the visible worlds on the Divine Process, and it had revealed to Him the mysterious manner whereby His Great Work would achieve Effectiveness. With the signs of the fulfillment of His Teaching Work in the Liberated confessions of true devotees, Swami Da Love-Ananda's Great Intention to Awaken living beings is being fulfilled. The "Dawn Horse" of an Awakened Community of true devotees is beginning to appear.

Advaitayana Buddhist Communion,[18] making public the alignment of Swami Da Love-Ananda's Way of Radical Understanding to the great traditions of Advaita Vedanta[19] and Buddhism. And Swami Da Love-Ananda founded the Free Order of Advaitayana Buddhist Renunciates[20] and the Hermitage Service Order.[21]

18. For a description of The Advaitayana Buddhist Communion and its unique affinities with the venerable sacred traditions of Advaitism and Buddhism, see "The Principle of Retreat" (pp. 281ff, below). Also, see especially Swami Da Love-Ananda's source Work, *Nirvanasara: Radical Transcendentalism and the Introduction of Advaitayana Buddhism.*

19. Advaita Vedanta (literally, "the non-dualistic end of the Vedas") is an ancient tradition of Hindu philosophy, based on the highest wisdom of the *Upanishads.* Its philosophy points to Reality or "Brahman" as transcendental and prior to all phenomena. Its highest Realization is that there is no distinction between the individual, the world, and Brahman or the Divine Reality.

20. The Free Order of Advaitayana Buddhist Renunciates is a celibate monastic order of The Advaitayana Buddhist Communion. Members of the Free Renunciate Order have in spirit renounced all worldly concerns, and they have legally renounced all ownership of property. They live in voluntary simplicity, generally residing at one or another of the Meditation Sanctuaries of the Communion. Members of the Free Renunciate Order serve the Heart-Master and His Agencies on behalf of the Communion. They also serve and maintain the Communion's Sanctuaries and provide various Spiritual, educational, and practical services (such as the preparation of literature, or the management of retreats) for the general membership of the Communion.

Members of the Free Renunciate Order practice the unique disciplines of the Radical or most direct form of the Way Taught by Da Love-Ananda Avadhoota. Thus, they demonstrate the most conservative discipline and the most intense practice of the Way, and they act as an inspiration to all others to likewise devote themselves fully to the Process of Divine Realization.

21. The Hermitage Service Order is the primary Agency of devotees within the general institutional Community who are charged with the

Advaitism and Buddhism are the two branches of the Great Tradition[22] with which Da Love-Ananda said He enjoys a Great Sympathy, since both of these traditions ultimately transcend themselves in the Realization of the seventh stage of life. Like Da Love-Ananda, the founders of these traditions, Adi Shankara[23] and

---

responsibility of carrying the Teaching and the Blessing of the Heart-Master to all devotees.

Members of the Hermitage Service Order are typically married couples who voluntarily embrace the discipline of motiveless celibacy as a sign of the Sufficiency of Realization and Heart-Communion with the True Heart-Master and the Divine Person. Though living in the general precincts of the Community of devotees, they otherwise embrace and exemplify the Radical practice and conservative renunciate disciplines lived by members of the Free Renunciate Order. Thus, effectively, they live in the spirit of Hermitage renunciation, and they demonstrate the principle of true renunciation and service.

22. The "Great Tradition" is Swami Da Love-Ananda's term for the total inheritance of religious, magical, Spiritual, and transcendental paths, philosophies, and testimonies from all the eras and cultures of humanity. Swami Da Love-Ananda has stated the relationship between His own Work and the Great Tradition as follows:

"All the great schools ultimately fulfill themselves in the seventh stage disposition. The Way that I Teach is the Way based on this seventh stage wisdom. This Teaching includes a critical commentary on the Great Tradition. We naturally feel that our moment of Spiritual culture is built upon or presumes the Great Tradition as its past. Not any one province or segment of the Great Tradition but the Great Tradition as a whole is our tradition. Yet we do not follow that Great Tradition dogmatically. We simply have an affinity for it, based on what we understand, in our consideration, to be the Way. Ours is an affinity based on critical understanding." ("The Seven Schools of God-Talk", preface to *The Song of the Self Supreme [Ashtavakra Gita],* translated by R. Mukerjee [San Rafael, Calif.: The Dawn Horse Press, 1982], p. 47.)

23. Shankara (A.D. 788-820), who is celebrated as the greatest philosophical genius of the Hindu tradition, created the ultimate expo-

Gautama, also reformed the ancient institutions of celibate renunciation.

Sri Da Love-Ananda's Great Sacrifice and the miraculous transformation of devotees is the story of what occurred at the Naitauba Hermitage in Fiji. Those who did "hear"[24] and "see"[25] Him leaped beyond limits and tendencies which had not been transcended even

---

sition of Advaita Vedanta, or unqualified non-dualism, according to which the world as it is ordinarily experienced is but a superimposition upon the One Reality. In Swami Da Love-Ananda's words, Shankara attempted "to construct a language of philosophy that is compatible with ultimate Realization". Shankara Taught the practice of inverting attention upon the self-Essence ("atman") to the point of perfect transcendence of object-awareness and coalescence with It. Before settling in Kanchi, he traveled throughout India, realigning the practice of ceremonial worship to actual contact with the Living Presence. In the "four corners" of India he established monasteries that exist to this day. Shankara founded ten orders of "sannyasins", collectively referred to as the "Dashanamis". The orders are: Saraswati, Puri, Bharati, Vana, Aranya, Tirtha, Asrama, Giri, Parvata, and Sagara.

24. In *The Dawn Horse Testament* (p. 304), Swami Da Love-Ananda describes "hearing" as follows:

"True 'Hearing' Involves Sensitivity To the conditional self, To The Point Of The Utter Conviction That the conditional self (or the conventional 'I') Is Contraction, and This To The Degree That It Is Obvious That No self-Manipulation Can Bring An End To self-Contraction. True Hearing Is Awakened When All Such Efforts Cease, and The Heart Naturally Opens Beyond self-Contraction Into The Effortless Disposition Of Love."

25. In *The Dawn Horse Testament* (p. 314), Swami Da Love-Ananda describes "seeing" as follows:

"Seeing Is Spontaneous (or Heart-Moved) Devotional Sacrifice Of the self-Contraction. Seeing Is The self-Transcending Reorientation Of conditional Existence To The Transcendental and Divine Spiritual Condition In Whom conditional self and conditional worlds arise and Always Already Inhere."

after many years of disciplined practice. Love-Ananda's Grand Victory, the Great Horse-Sacrifice, had accomplished what fifteen years of progressive practice had not. It was only after testing and observing the signs of Radical Understanding in devotees that He revealed that the Great Event in January had been the fulfillment of the great "Ashvamedha"[26] Sacrifice, as He had prophesied in the conclusion to *The Dawn Horse Testament*.

I Am The Horse-Sacrifice, The "Ashvamedha", Whereby The Truth and The Power Of Transcendental Divine Self-Realization Are Transmitted To The Cosmic Mandala[27] *Of beings![28]*

Three thousand years ago, the forest Teachings of the ancient Indian Seers, or "Rishis", revealed a Spiritual Mystery ("Rahasya") they called the Ashvamedha,

26. The Indian horse-sacrifice (Sanskrit: "ashvamedha") is a complex ceremony with many levels of meaning and purpose. As it is commonly understood, it was principally a religio-magical rite performed only by the greatest of India's "rajas". However, the common or exoteric interpretations of the horse-sacrifice are not at all the great Ashvamedha, which the legendary Rishis proclaimed to be the greatest of all sacrifices. The true Horse-Sacrifice is the Cosmic Sacrifice performed by the Transcendental Divine Self, whereby a Divinely Realized Adept is Incarnated with the Power and Purpose of re-establishing the Teaching and Way of Transcendental Self-Realization.

27. The Sanskrit word "mandala" is a traditional term that literally means "circle". For Swami Da Love-Ananda's complete consideration of the Cosmic Mandala, or the totality of the manifest cosmos, see chapter 39 of *The Dawn Horse Testament*. Please also see Master Da's instructions in *Easy Death: Talks and Essays on the Inherent and Ultimate Transcendence of Death and Everything Else*.

28. Da Free John [Swami Da Love-Ananda Paramahansa Avadhoota], *The Dawn Horse Testament* (San Rafael, Calif.: The Dawn Horse Press, 1985), p. 699.

or "Horse-Sacrifice". The Ashvamedha was said to be "the greatest of all Sacrifices", and it remained the focus of contemplation for the ancient Seers, who handed on its inner meaning only to the "tested few". For millennia since the Vedic era, the true significance of the Rishis' Spiritual Riddle has remained secret.

In 1976, Swami Da Love-Ananda handed me a small orange card on which He had written the words "Horse-Sacrifice, Ashvamedha", and suggested this might be a good title for a book on the Sacred History of His Teaching Work. The next day, however, Love-Ananda told me it was not yet the right time to use the title. Shortly after this incident, I received an unsolicited letter from a Dutch scholar in Ceylon, explaining that he had shown a copy of *The Laughing Man* magazine[29] to a Spiritual teacher named Swami Siva Kalki. When asked to comment on Bubba Free John (Heart-Master Da Love-Ananda's name during His early Teaching years), the Swami had given a remarkable answer:

To understand Bubba Free John one should know the Vedas; for unless one understands the Vedic Horse, one cannot understand the implications of what his appearance truly means.

When asked to explain further, the Swami only said:

It means that someone's Vedic "Yajna" ("sacrifice") has been successful. More than that would require an

---

29. *The Laughing Man: The Alternative to Scientific Materialism and Religious Provincialism* is a quarterly journal published by The Advaitayana Buddhist Communion.

*initiate to comprehend. It is enough to say that Bubba
Free John is the Dawn Horse himself.*[30]

The Ashvamedha, or Great Horse-Sacrifice of the
Transcendental Being, requires the complete submission of a human agency if the Transcendental Divine
Self is to effectively assume a human conditional state.
If the sacrifice is accomplished, the Transcendental
Self has found a direct means in human likeness
through which to Transmit Its own Condition to
human beings. Thus, Love-Ananda's submission to
human birth required that He assume *all* the conditions human beings suffer and indulge. The great
struggle of His Teaching years was in effect the process
of the Incarnation of the Divine Self, which culminated
in the Victorious Event in Fiji.

Only the Great Power of the Ashvamedha, truly
accomplished, is effectively and really Liberating. This
is the secret reason why the appearance of a "World-
Teacher" was so highly cherished in esoteric circles of
the East. Many yogis, saints, and sages have entered the
human plane to serve the Spiritual needs of mankind.
But those endowed with the Siddhi to *really* Liberate
others are extremely rare, for the Liberation of others
is the Work of the "Mahasiddha",[31] the Great Adept or
World-Master.

30. Comments by Swami Siva Kalki, recorded by A. M. Verreyen. From
Mr. Verreyen's correspondence with The Laughing Man Institute,
August 12, 1977, quoted by Saniel Bonder in "Attend to the
Liberator", *Crazy Wisdom,* vol. 1, no. 5 (August 1982), p. 17.

31. The Sanskrit term "Siddha" literally means a "Completed, Fulfilled, or Perfect One". A Siddha is one who is Perfectly Awakened to

45

This secret knowledge of the Ashvamedha was carefully guarded by the Rishis, who suspected, and rightly so, that non-initiates of the mysteries of sacred knowledge would wrongly adhere to a magical, conventional, or exoteric interpretation of the highly esoteric and world-transcending Ashvamedha. Such exoteric, conventional, and cultic renderings of the great Spiritual mysteries wrongly presume there is no need for concentrated practice ("sadhana"), true devotion, renunciation, and all the tribulations and glories of a life of sacrifice on the part of those who receive Grace.

Nothing could be further from the truth. As the history of Da Love-Ananda's Teaching Work reveals, there is an absolute necessity for personal responsibility, or submission to the Way of Divine Grace. A life of renunciation, real meditation, and discipline must coincide with the necessary Gift of Spiritual and Transcendental Help and Realization. The cause of the Rishis' praise and safeguarding of the Ashvamedha was that they knew the Adept's Supreme Yoga was the "means", the Gift of Grace, Freely Given, whereby their practice could be fulfilled in perfect Realization. Thus it was said that "men did not know the way to the heavenly world, but the horse did." Love-Ananda's Great Event was the sign of the Sacrifice of the "Horse", or the Incarnated Adept, who leads all those

---

or Identified with Radiant Transcendental Consciousness. The "Mahasiddha" is the "Great Realizer" functioning for the sake of living beings as a Realized Adept endowed with the capacity to Transmit the "Siddhi" of Radiant Transcendental Consciousness to others.

who "hear" and "see" to the Realization of Love-Ananda.

With the completion of His Sacrifice, Da Love-Ananda now points to His *Love-Ananda Gita,* wherein He says that the practice is to simply "hear Perfectly" and "see Perfectly". Via this practice, devotees duplicate the Consciousness of Sri Da Love-Ananda. Love-Ananda's Incomprehensible Yoga of duplication, whereby beings are Liberated by the Divine Being, is the secret and the result of the ancient Ashvamedha, and it is this same means of Grace that is being offered in our time.

With His Teaching Work and the writing of the *Love-Ananda Gita* finished, and the many auspicious Signs of practice and renunciation awakened in Hermitage members of the Free Renunciate Order, Love-Ananda was moved to be with devotees again. Owning nothing, attached to no one, without interest or concern for ordinary life, neither a householder, nor a public man, nor an institutional man, belonging to no creed or country, yet embracing the whole world in His Universal Love—such is the Free Renunciation of Da Love-Ananda Avadhoota, a true sannyasin, an eternal swan ("Paramahansa") or preserver of mankind. He journeyed to The Mountain of Attention Sanctuary in northern California to magnify His faculty of Universal Blessing, and through His "mere Presence" is granting dispassion ("vairagya"), renunciation ("tyaga"), and countless advantages to all living beings.

The Grand Victory has been accomplished, and the

Supreme Yoga is established on Earth. The Sign of Da Love-Ananda Paramahansa's Horse-Sacrifice is the Sign of the Supreme Yoga of the Divine Adept, whose own "reunion" with the Divine is inevitable, but Who must then perform the Supreme Yoga or the accomplishment of the reunion of everyone and the Divine.

This is the Mystery behind the ancient Ashvamedha: The "Horse" of manifest Enlightenment is the living Master, whose "Crazy" Invocation through submission to the world evokes and Awakens devotees to the elegant simplicity of Renunciation and Realization of Love-Ananda, the Love-Bliss of Consciousness.

The *Love-Ananda Gita* is a unique book in the long history of religious and Spiritual communication. It is one of the very few seventh stage Teaching texts ever written, and the only book that describes the transitional process and practice from the sixth to the seventh stage of life. Its Radical message intentionally does not support, suggest, or accommodate any practice or point of view belonging to the first five stages of life. Even the orientation to the sixth stage of life is presented within the context of the seventh or perfect stage of life.

As Swami Da Love-Ananda Paramahansa argues throughout the *Love-Ananda Gita*, the struggle of the progressive approach to Realization is not necessary. This is certainly one of the paradoxes of Spiritual life, but the fact remains that Love-Ananda's Radical practice can be taken up sooner and fulfilled more quickly than the progressive and apparently less demanding approach to Realization. The progressive or gradual approach to Realization can take many years before one begins to approximate anything even comparable to the discipline of "Feeling-Enquiry" and the Free Renunciation described in the *Love-Ananda Gita*.

Thus, with His *Love-Ananda Gita*, it is now known that the most Radical approach to Realization Taught by Da Love-Ananda Avadhoota is also the simplest and the most Happy. The Great Lesson that Da Love-Ananda has demonstrated to devotees is this: Any accommodation of the motivations associated with the first five stages of life is an accommodation of egoity, and therefore a choice to struggle with oneself and to delay the course of Realization.

Swami Da Love-Ananda's Grand Victory in Hermitage Naitauba, where He Taught the Great Lesson of Renunciation and Liberation by Grace, was the fulfillment of His lifelong Mission to bring His Radical Way of Understanding into the Consciousness of humanity.

Now, with His offering of the *Love-Ananda Gita*, Swami Da Love-Ananda Paramahansa has handed on the new tradition and "Radical" Understanding of Advaitayana Buddhism to those of His "hearers" who are entirely devoted to the Realization of Truth in their own Being.

He who gifts others with this *Love-Ananda Gita*, offered with compassion, benefits the communication of Truth and the Spiritual healing of the world. Other sacred texts of the Great Tradition have shined in their time, and the greatest of these still hold the Truth hidden within them today. But the *Love-Ananda*

Gita makes obvious the Secrets that remained hidden within the traditions, and newly presents the Ancient Way of the Great Heart-Master.

Devotees of the Conscious Heart, whose desire for Truth is nurtured here, never seek for Love-Ananda outside the heart again. Heart-Realization is to all other attainments what the Lion is to all other animals, the Great Ocean to other waters, and the Heart-Master to other men. As the Sun is unequalled amongst celestial bodies in showering light upon the Earth, so does this *Love-Ananda Gita* shine among sacred literature in Enlightening the whole body of Man.

Love-Ananda Gita, the Heart-Book, precious to those who worship Consciousness Itself, celebrates that Supreme Being, Brilliant, and Conscious, Whose Name is Da. For anyone who "hears" this Song of Da Love-Ananda and who "sees" the Dawn Horse Master through the eyes of devotion, for that fortunate man, the search for Truth is ended.

Oh men and women of today, why not meditate on that Person, Bright and Open-Eyed, Who, untroubled by desire and death, lit the lamp of non-dual Wisdom for men in times past, and Who through Grace grants that Light in ours and every generation. Give thanks with me to the Crazy Wise Man, Da, the exalted Renunciate, the likes of Whom the Western world has never known in the flesh, Who willingly sacrificed the Horse of Self for all beings and said, "Be dyed in my color of Renunciation and Realization."

Let us hold up our hands to Sri Da Love-Ananda Paramahansa Avadhoota, the Laughing Man, Who, saddled upon the Dawn Horse of spontaneous Teaching, rides through the Mandala of space and time, saying, "Now I Have Revealed My Mystery To You. Consider It Fully, and Then Choose What You Will Do."

Swami Daji Ashvamedhananda Muliwai
The Mountain of Attention Sanctuary

LOVE-ANANDA GITA
(The Free-Song of Love-Bliss)

The "Perfect Summary"
of "Radical"
Advaitayana Buddhism

by
Swami Da Love-Ananda
Paramahansa Avadhoota
(Heart-Master Da Free John)

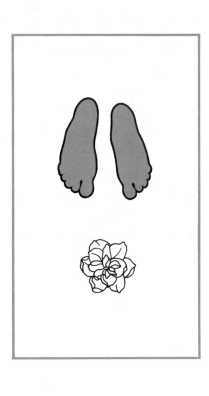

1.

When I Began To Teach, I Taught Only the "Radical"[1] (or Most Direct) Process of self-Transcendence (or Transcendence of the self-Contraction) and Immediate Realization of the Transcendental Divine Self-Condition.

2.

I Summarized My Description (and Realization) of That "Radical" or Most Direct Process In *The Knee of Listening*.

3.

Then I Called My "Listeners"[2] To "Merely Observe" (or Simply To "Witness") the total body-mind itself and <u>all</u> "things" (or all conditional phenomena).

4.

I Called My "Listeners" To Stand <u>As</u> the "Witness-Consciousness" and To "Merely Observe" all conditions associated with the "first five stages of life",[3] all "gross" (or physical) and "subtle" (or etheric and mental) phenomena of the "frontal line" and the "spinal line" of the body-mind, or all experience and knowledge of the "Circle"[4] of the "Spirit-Current".

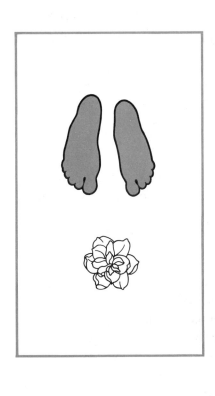

5.

I Called My "Listeners" To "Witness" the "Traditional Error"[5] associated with the "causal knot"[6] (or Primal egoic Stress and Illusion) in the "sixth stage of life", which is the Tendency To Presume that Consciousness is Either separate, independent, personal, phenomenal, conditional, and limited, Or, If Transcendental and Unlimited, Yet Unable To "Recognize"[7] (or To Directly and Immediately Transcend) the body-mind and the world as they arise.

6.

I Called My "Listeners" To Realize the "seventh stage of life", or, By the "Radical" or Most Direct Process of "Consideration"[8] of Reality, To Realize the Spiritual, Transcendental, and Divine Condition of Consciousness Itself, Inherently Transcending and Immediately "Recognizing" the total body-mind itself and all "things".

7.

I Called My "Listeners" To "Witness" the "I" of the body-mind.

8.

I Called My "Listeners" To Observe that the total body-mind <u>itself</u> is the "I", or the ego.

9.

I Called My "Listeners" To Observe that the ego-"I", or the body-mind itself, is "Narcissus",[9] or the complex "Habit" of the <u>avoidance</u> of relationship.

10.

I Called My "Listeners" To Observe that the ego, or the separate and personal "I", or the body-mind itself, is <u>Simply</u> and <u>Only</u> the activity of self-Contraction.

11.

I Said: Observe and Understand.

12.

I Said: <u>All</u> that arises as experience and knowledge is merely self-Contraction, the avoidance of relationship, the Illusion of separateness, or the self-Deluded and separative "Habit of Narcissus".

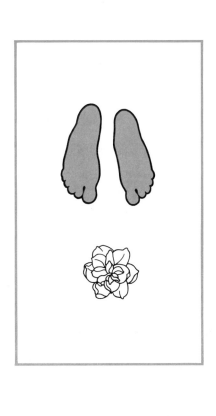

I Said: <u>All</u> that arises as experience and
knowledge is an Illusion of separated urgency,
dis-ease and need, painful desire, painful
reaction, fleet pleasure, painful addiction, painful
frustration, inevitable anger, sorrow, fear, and
death, and Seeking for More and Less.

I Said: Since <u>all</u> that arises is merely a Suffered
Illusion of self-Contraction, or Un-Happiness, the
Way of Happiness Is to Transcend self-
Contraction, At its Root or Heart.

I Said: Therefore, Transcend self-Contraction At
the Heart, In Consciousness Itself.

I Said: In the "first five stages of life", attention
Moves Outwardly, descending and then
ascending In the "Circle" of "objects" and
"others" (or <u>all</u> "things"), and <u>Any</u> Submission of
attention to the "things" of the "first five stages
of life" Intensifies self-Contraction (or the ego-
"I") and Perpetuates the Agonized Search for
self-Fulfillment and self-Release.

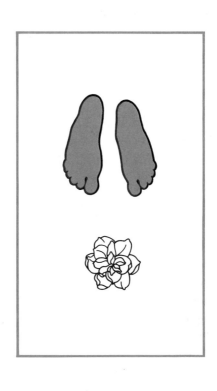

17

I Said: In the "first five stages of life", attention
Seeks for the body "things", the "things" of
mind, and the "thing itself" (Above and Beyond
the body-mind), and Any Accommodation of the
apparent needs, limitations, Searches, or "things"
of the "first five stages of life" is an Embrace of
time and death, a Concession to More (and
More) Struggle with self-Contraction, and an
Agreement to Delay (Even Perpetually) the
"Perfect Realization" of God, Truth, Reality, or
Happiness.

18.

I Said: In the "sixth stage of life", attention
Collapses on itself, In its Place of Origin, Prior To
all "things" and All Seeking (Above and Beyond).

19.

I Said: In the "sixth stage of life", attention
Subsides and Is Resolved In its Transcendental or
"Subjective" Source, the Transcendental Heart [10]
That Is Consciousness Itself.

20.

I Said: In the "seventh stage of life", the Self-
Radiant Heart That Is Consciousness Itself Stands
Free, As Itself.

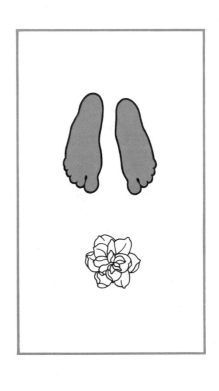

21.

I Said: In the "seventh stage of life", all
conditions Freely and Spontaneously arise, but
attention Cannot Bind the Self-Radiant
Consciousness, and all "things" Fade In the
Enormous Light of Inherent and Self-Existing
Being.

22.

I Said: Therefore, Be Free of the "Circle" and <u>All</u>
the Illusions of attention to the body-mind and
the "things" of the "first five stages of life".

23.

I Said: Be Free of the Disease that is attention
itself.

24.

I Said: The Way that I Teach Is the Way of
"Radical" Understanding.

25.

I Said: What is to be Understood is attention
itself.

26.

I Said: Attention is self-Contraction, and all
"objects" and "others" (or all "things") are its
Illusions.

65

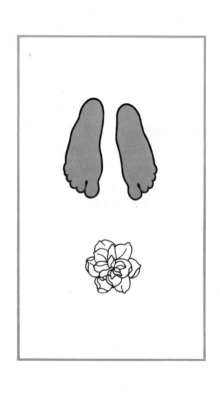

27.

I Said: Practice of the Way that I Teach Is Release of the Motive that Moves to "things".

28.

I Said: Practice of the Way that I Teach Is To Stand Free of "things" and To Swoon In Consciousness Itself.

29.

I Said: Therefore, Let attention Collapse from the "Circle" of "things" and Fall to Infinity In the "Heart-Current" of "Merely Being".

30.

I Said: There Is Infinite Inherent Happiness, There In the Well of "Merely Being".

31.

I Said: The Inherent Happiness of "Merely Being" Is Countlessly "Brighter" (or More Radiantly Blissful) than the "Circular" Worlds of Fascinated separation.

32.

I Said: Therefore, Eat attention In the Heart.

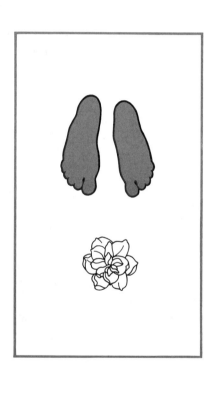

I Said: Attention (or all of mind) is Always an act of identification with some limitation or limited "state".

I Said: Therefore, Stand Free, Before the mind Makes a "Difference".

I Said: Stand and Be, Free of Motive and "object" and "other" and "thing".

I Said: Shed the Disease of separation and Seeking.

I Said: Be Healed of the Illusion of "other" and "empty".

I Said: Be Healed of all "things" By the Heart Of "Love-Ananda".

I Said: Understand and Release all "things" In the Radiant Feel Of "Love-Ananda", Who Is Consciousness Itself.

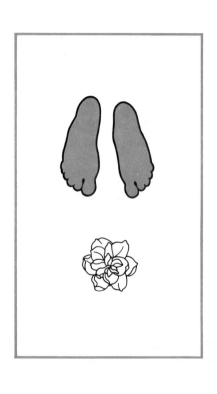

40.

I Said: All that arises is an apparent modification of the Inherent Radiance of Consciousness Itself.

41.

I Said: All that arises is "things" of attention.

42.

I Said: Therefore, all that arises is <u>only</u> mind, or thought, or concept.

43.

I Said: You experience or know every "thing" In Consciousness Itself.

44.

I Said: Therefore, all "things" are <u>only</u> the apparent mind of Consciousness Itself.

45.

I Said: All that is to be Transcended is In Consciousness Itself.

46.

I Said: Therefore, what is to be Transcended is the Process of mind, or thinking.

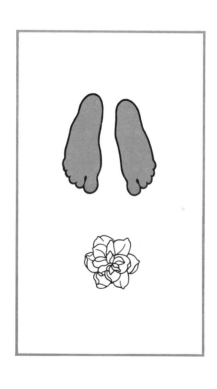

47.

I Said: Attention is the essence of mind itself and every thought.

48.

I Said: Therefore, what is to be Transcended is attention itself.

49.

I Said: Even the ego-"I" is merely an "object", or an "other", or a "thing" of attention.

50.

I Said: The ego-"I" is only a thought.

51.

I Said: The "I" is only the ego, Until the ego is Transcended.

52.

I Said: The "I", as the ego, is only self-Contraction.

53.

I Said: The ego-"I", or self-Contraction, is the body-mind.

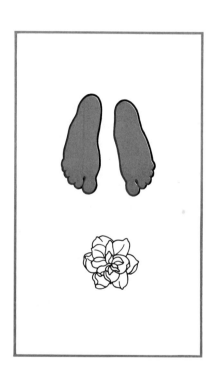

I Said: The ego-"I", the self-Contraction, or the total body-mind, is <u>only</u> a thought.

I Said: The ego-"I" is not only Contraction <u>of</u> the body-mind, but it is Contraction <u>as</u> the body-mind.

I Said: The ego-"I", or the self-Contraction, <u>is</u> the body-mind itself, and Not merely a "someone" Behind or Within the body-mind.

I Said: Therefore, if egoity is to be Transcended, it is the body-mind itself that <u>Must</u> be Transcended.

I Said: The body-mind is a dependent "form", arising in <u>Necessary</u> Unity with the Totality of Conditional Nature (or <u>all</u> actual and potential causes and effects).

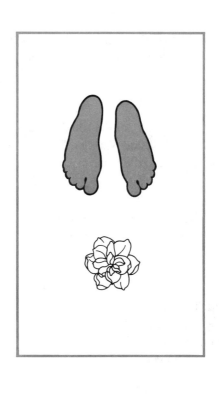

I Said: Because the dependent body-mind is Always Already in Unity with All of Conditional Nature, there is No Need to be born In Order To Achieve Unity with Conditional Nature (high or low).

I Said: Therefore, You are Not born In Order To Seek and Achieve Unity with any "state" or plane of Conditional Nature.

I Said: Birth and death are merely the Consequences of Prior Unity with All of Conditional Nature, Rather Than a Means To Achieve Unity with All or a part of Conditional Nature.

I Said: Therefore, birth and experience and knowledge and death are Not merely to be Sought, or Attained, or Suffered.

I Said: Birth and experience and knowledge and death are to be Transcended.

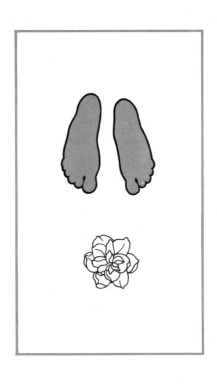

64.

I Said: The body-mind is Inherently related to All (and every part) of Conditional Nature.

65.

I Said: Therefore, the body-mind, or the ego-"I", or the self-Contraction, or the <u>avoidance</u> of relationship, is itself relatedness, or relationship itself.

66.

I Said: The ego-"I" is a Paradox of relationship and separation.

67.

I Said: The ego-"I" is the Image of relatedness itself.

68.

I Said: The ego-"I" is also the Image of separation, or relationlessness.

69.

I Said: The ego-"I" is "Narcissus", or the <u>Illusion</u> of the body-mind.

70.

I Said: The ego-"I" is "Narcissus", or the <u>Illusion</u> of the self-Contraction.

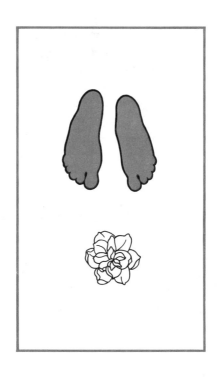

71.

I Said: The ego-"I" is "Narcissus", or the <u>Illusion</u> of the avoidance of relationship.

72.

I Said: The ego-"I" is "Narcissus", or the <u>Illusion</u> of relationship and relatedness and separation and separateness and separativeness and relationlessness.

73.

I Said: In Consciousness Itself, There is No Such "thing" as the ego-"I", or "Narcissus", or the self-Contraction, or the avoidance of relationship.

74.

I Said: In Consciousness Itself, There is No Such "thing" as relationship, or relatedness, or separation, or separateness, or separativeness, or relationlessness.

75.

I Said: In Consciousness Itself, There is No Such "thing" as the body-mind, or the "other", or any "object".

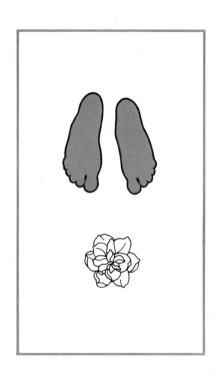

76.

I Said: The ego-"I", "Narcissus", or the self-Contraction, is <u>only</u> a thought, or a thoughtless feeling.

77.

I Said: The avoidance of relationship is <u>only</u> a thought, or a thoughtless feeling.

78.

I Said: Relationship, relatedness, separation, separateness, separativeness, or relationlessness, is <u>only</u> a thought, or a thoughtless feeling.

79.

I Said: Even the body-mind itself is <u>totally</u> and <u>only</u> a thought, or a thoughtless feeling.

80.

I Said: Attention <u>Must</u> be "Turned About" (or Relaxed) from mind, thought, thoughtless feeling, perception, "object", and "other", or all "things", and Resolved In its Transcendental or "Subjective" Source, Which Is Consciousness Itself.

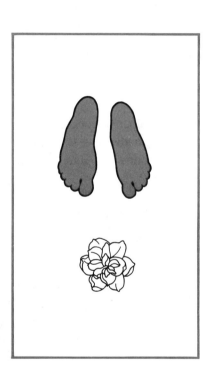

81.

I Said: Therefore, Understand and Release all "things" In Consciousness Itself, Via the Agency of "Love-Ananda", the mindless or thoughtless and Inherent or Transcendental Feeling of Heart-Bliss, Who "I" <u>Am</u>.

82.

I Said: Those Who "Hear" Me [11] Understand and Relinquish the self-Contraction, and Those Who "See" Me Are Blessed With Awakening To the Free Love-Bliss, or Eternal Happiness, of Inherent Being.

83.

I Said: Therefore, "Hear" Me (or <u>Understand</u> Your conditional "self") and "See" Me (or <u>Transcend</u> Your conditional "self"), and So Be Moved To Stand Free of the "first five stages of life", In the Place of the "Witness-Consciousness", Where Even the "sixth stage of life" is to be Transcended.

84.

I Said: "Hear" Me and "See" Me, and So Be Moved To Stand Prior To the body-mind.

85.

I Said: Stand <u>As</u> You <u>Are</u>, and So <u>Be</u> Free.

85

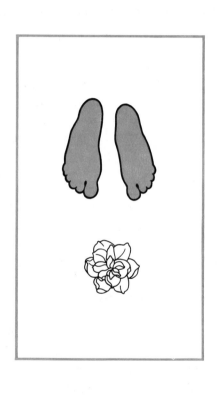

I Said: The One Who Says All of This To You <u>Is</u> the Heart, Who Transcends the "things".

87.

Even So, and Even Though It Was So Given, It Soon Became Clear That My Devotees Were Not Prepared For This "Radical" or Most Direct Process of Realization.

88.

Therefore, In Response to the needs and limitations and "stages of life" of Those Who came to Me, I Became Spontaneously Moved to a Unique Ordeal of Teaching.

89.

That Ordeal Was Based On a "Crazy Method".

90.

My Devotees Revealed to Me that They Were Not Immediately Able To Submit (or Give) Themselves To Me (In the Traditional Devotional Manner).

91.

Therefore, I Gave (or Submitted) Myself To Them, Constantly (In the Manner of a Sacrificial Offering).

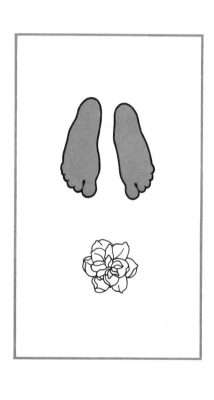

92.

By Means of This Ordeal, I Gradually Developed the Progressive (but Still Direct) Way that I Teach.

93.

I have Summarized That Progressive (and Direct) Way that I Teach In *The Dawn Horse Testament*.

94.

Now That Great Teaching Ordeal Has Completed Itself, and I Have Retired Into Hermitage Seclusion.

95.

I have Affirmed and Effected the Completion of My Teaching Ordeal By Spontaneously Embracing the Signs of "Sannyas", or Great Renunciation, In the Always Already Free Manner of an "Avadhoota".

96.

Therefore, I Have Returned from the world To the "Only" Place I Never Left.

97.

Here In My Space of No More Work, I Speak Only of the "Radical" or Most Direct Process of Transcendence of the self-Contraction and Immediate Realization of the Transcendental Divine Self-Condition.

98.

In the Progressive (but Still Direct) Form of My Teaching, I Constantly Submitted To My Devotees, and I Made a Constant Response to the "point of view" of All My "Listeners".

99.

In the "Radical" or Most Direct Form of My Teaching, I Only Speak My Own "Point of View", Which Is the Ultimate (and "Perfect") "Point of View" (or Heart) of all conditionally manifested beings.

100.

Now I Will Make My "Perfect Summary" of the "Radical" or Most Direct Way that I Teach.

101.

I Am Heart-Master Da Love-Ananda, the "True Heart-Master" of My Devotees.

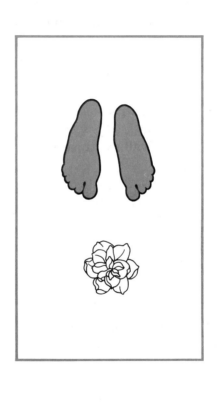

102.

I Am "Da" (the "Giver"), Who Gives.

103.

I Am "Love-Ananda", What Is, and What Is Given.

104.

I Am the "Heart", Where "I AM" [12] Is To Be
Found.

105.

Realization of Who, What, and Where "I AM" Is
Realization of Me.

106.

The Secret (or Hidden Meaning) of My Name Is
the Free Heart-Gift of "Love-Ananda", Inherent
Love-Bliss, or Happiness Itself.

107.

Happiness Itself (or "Love-Ananda") Is the
"True Heart-Master" (Who I Am).

108.

Therefore, In every moment, "Remember" [13] (or
Locate and Commune With) Me, At (and Via)
Your Feeling-Heart, and As Happiness Itself.

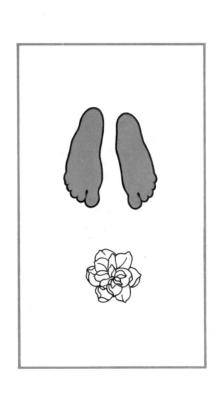

109.

If You Will "Hear" Me and "See" Me Most "Perfectly", "Radically", or Directly, You Will Realize "Love-Ananda", or Happiness Itself.

110.

Heart-Realization of "Love-Ananda", or Inherent Love-Bliss, or Happiness Itself, Is "Perfect" Devotion To Me.

111.

The Way that I Teach Is "Love-Ananda", or Happiness Itself.

112.

Therefore, My Ultimate Secret Is In My Name.

113.

My Ultimate Secret Is My Name Itself.

114.

My Name Is In (or At) Your Heart.

115.

Therefore, the Heart Is Mine.

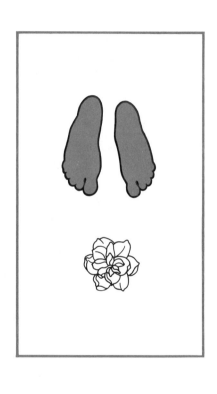

116.

I Am the Heart.

117.

Your Heart Is Me.

118.

The Heart Itself Is "Love-Ananda", or Happiness Itself.

119.

Every being is Constantly Seeking Happiness.

120.

You are Constantly Seeking Happiness.

121.

Even though You are Constantly Seeking Happiness, You Are Happiness Itself.

122.

Only Happiness Itself Is Free of the Need to Seek Happiness.

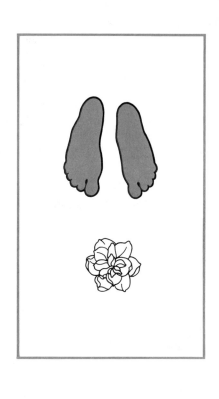

123.

If <u>Only</u> Happiness Itself is Chosen, Soon all else is Forgotten.

124.

Therefore, Be <u>Exclusively</u> and "<u>Perfectly</u>" Devoted To Happiness Itself.

125.

Do This By <u>Renouncing</u> (and Thus Transcending) every "thing" (or all "objects", all experience, all knowledge, all relations, and all "others"), or <u>all</u> that is Not Happiness Itself.

126.

In every moment, Locate Happiness Itself, Realize Happiness Itself, and <u>Be</u> Happiness Itself.

127.

Locate Happiness Itself By Feeling the Native Feeling In Which all "other" feelings, thoughts, perceptions, and sensations are apparently arising.

128.

Realization of God, Truth, or Reality Itself <u>Is</u> Liberation.

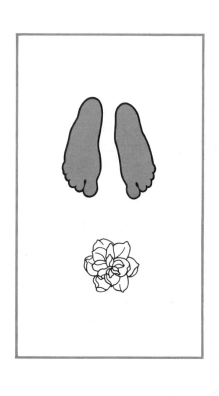

129.

Realization of Happiness Itself Is Realization of God, Truth, or Reality Itself.

130.

Therefore, Realize Happiness Itself.

131.

The Way that I Teach Is the Way of What Is (or Who Is), Where and As Only One (and No "Other") Is.

132.

The Only One That Obviously Is (When the Illusion of separateness and "things" is Directly or Inherently Transcended) Is the Way that I Teach.

133.

To "Remember" (or Commune With) the Only One That Is, "Merely" (or Directly and Inherently) Realize What Is, Where and As It Is.

134.

To "Remember" (or Commune With) the One That Is, Simply (or "Merely") Be Who, What, and Where You Are.

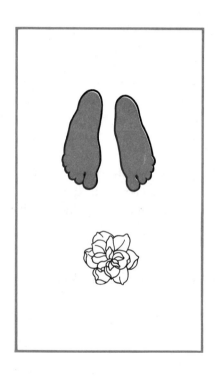

135.

Only "Remember" (or <u>Realize</u>) Your Self, or the Heart Itself, <u>As</u> "I <u>AM</u>" (or <u>As</u> the Inherent or Self-Existing Feeling of "Merely Being").

136.

"I <u>AM</u>" (or Being Itself) <u>Is</u> Transcendental Self-Awareness (or Consciousness Itself).

137.

The "True Heart-Master" <u>Is</u> Consciousness Itself, Awakening You To Itself.

138.

Therefore, Locate and Realize Me, <u>As</u> Inherent and Inherently Free Self-Awareness, or Consciousness Itself.

139.

Locate and Realize Consciousness Itself, Prior To attention and the "objects" and "others" (or "things") of attention.

140.

Locate and Realize Consciousness Itself, By Not Seeking attention and its "objects", "others", or "things".

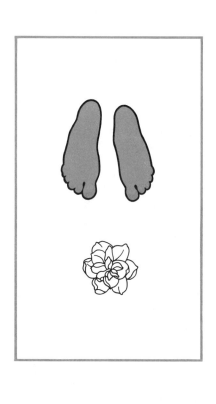

141.

Locate and Realize Consciousness Itself, By "Merely Witnessing" (and Not identifying with) attention and its "objects", "others", or "things".

142.

Locate and Realize Consciousness Itself, By Freely Relaxing, Releasing, and Dissolving attention (and its "objects", "others", or "things") In Consciousness Itself.

143.

Locate and Realize Consciousness Itself, By Feeling (and Thus Locating and Realizing) "Love-Ananda", Inherent Love-Bliss, or Happiness Itself.

144.

God Is Who, Truth Is What, and Reality Is Where You Always Already Are.

145.

God, Truth, or Reality Is Who, What, and Where You Are Before self-Contraction and its relations are apparently Added to Who, What, and Where You Are.

146.

God, Truth, or Reality "Merely" (or Only) Is.

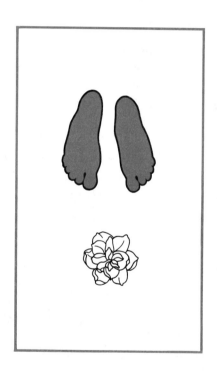

147.

Therefore, God, Truth, or Reality Is Existence Itself, or Inherent Being.

148.

Consciousness Is.

149.

Consciousness Itself "Merely" and Only Is.

150.

Consciousness Itself Is Only Self-Aware.

151.

Consciousness Itself (As Itself) Cannot be Reduced to some "thing" else, or Divided into parts, or Produced as an effect of any cause, or Destroyed as an effect of any cause, Nor Can It In Any Manner be Preceded or Interrupted or Followed by any "object", or any "other", or any "thing" At All.

152.

Therefore, Consciousness Itself Exists Inherently, As Itself.

153.

Consciousness Itself Is Inherent Being, Self-Existence, or Existence Itself.

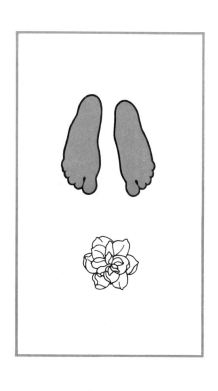

154.

Therefore, Consciousness Itself (As Itself) Is God, Truth, or Reality.

155.

God, Truth, or Reality Is the Source, the Point of Origin, or the Original Condition of what arises and What Is.

156.

Who, What, and Where Is the God, the Truth, and the Reality of the body?

157.

The ego-"I" (or the self-Contraction) is the body itself.

158.

The Source, the Point of Origin, or the Original Condition of the ego-"I" (or the self-Contraction) Is At the Heart.

159.

Therefore, the Heart Is the God, the Truth, and the Reality of the body.

160.

Who, What, and Where Is the God, the Truth, and the Reality of the mind?

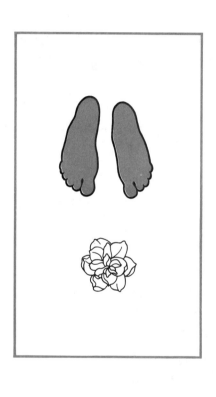

161.

The energy and the flow of thoughts is the mind itself.

162.

The Source, the Point of Origin, or the Original Condition of the energy and the flow of thoughts <u>Is</u> the "Spirit-Current", or the Energy and the Flow of "Love-Ananda", Love-Bliss, or Happiness Itself.

163.

Therefore, Happiness Itself <u>Is</u> the God, the Truth, and the Reality of the mind.

164.

The mind is the functional "subject" (or conditional self) of the body.

165.

Therefore, the mind is senior to the body.

166.

The "Spirit-Current" of Happiness Itself <u>Is</u> At the Heart of the body and At the Source of the mind.

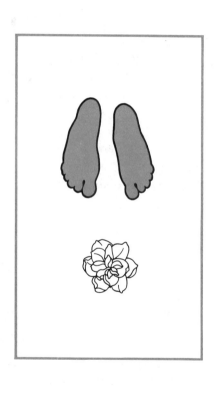

167.

Therefore, the "Heart-Current" of Happiness Itself Is the God, the Truth, and the Reality of the total body-mind.

168.

Who, What, and Where Is the God of Consciousness Itself?

169.

Consciousness Itself Is the Ultimate "Subject" (or Transcendental Self) of the body and the mind (or the total body-mind).

170.

Consciousness Itself Is Always Already Prior To the body-mind (or Inherently Without psycho-physical content).

171.

Only Consciousness Itself Is Consciousness Itself.

172.

The Source, the Point of Origin, or the Original Condition of Consciousness Itself Cannot Be "Other" than (or separate from) Consciousness Itself.

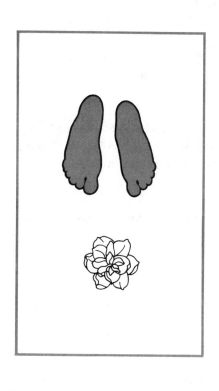

173.

Therefore, the Source, the Point of Origin, or the Original Condition of Consciousness Itself Is Consciousness Itself.

174.

Consciousness Itself Is the God, the Truth, and the Reality of Consciousness Itself.

175.

Consciousness Itself Is the Heart (or the Transcendental Self of the ego-"I").

176.

Therefore, Consciousness Itself Is the God, the Truth, and the Reality of the body.

177.

Consciousness Itself Is the Transcendental Self of the "Spirit-Current" of "Love-Ananda", Love-Bliss, or Happiness Itself.

178.

Therefore, Consciousness Itself Is the God, the Truth, and the Reality of the mind.

179.

Whatever arises to, in, or as the body or the mind arises To, In, and As Consciousness Itself.

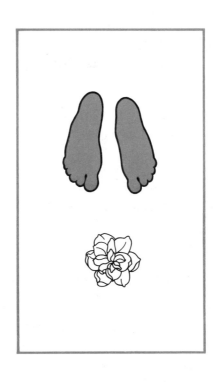

180.

Therefore, Consciousness Itself Is the God, the Truth, and the Reality of all "objects" and all "others" (or all "things").

181.

Only Consciousness Itself Is, While all else Only "seems".

182.

Whatever arises is Only a brief Illusion of attention, or an apparent modification of Consciousness Itself.

183.

Therefore, Consciousness Itself Is the Source, the Point of Origin, the Original Condition, the God, the Truth, and the Reality of What Is and what arises.

184.

Consciousness Is (Really or Inherently) Only Existing, Being, or Standing As itself, Aware Only Of Itself.

185.

"Da" Is Consciousness Itself, Standing As Itself.

186.

Consciousness Itself Is Your Very Self, or Self-Existence Itself, or Inherent Being, or the Inherent Feeling (or Feeling-Acknowledgment) of Being.

187.

Consciousness Itself Is "Love-Ananda", Inherent Love-Bliss, or Happiness Itself.

188.

Consciousness Itself Is To Be Located In (or Realized Via) the Under-Lying "Spirit-Current" (or the Inherent Feeling of Being) Associated With the right side of the Heart. [14]

189.

Consciousness Itself Is the "Spirit-Current", or the Inherent Feeling of Being, Which Is "Love-Ananda", Inherent Love-Bliss, or Happiness Itself.

190.

Who, What, and Where Is Consciousness Itself?

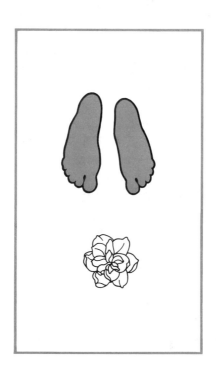

191.

Who, What, and Where Is the Inherent Feeling of Being, or Existence Itself?

192.

Who, What, and Where Is "Love-Ananda", Inherent Love-Bliss, or Happiness Itself?

193.

All My Devotees Should Ponder and Satisfy These Great Questions.

194.

All My Devotees Are Devotees of the Divine Truth and Reality That Is the Who, the What, and the Where of All the Great Questions.

195.

God, Truth, or Reality Is "Da".

196.

"Da" Is Self-Existing Being, Consciousness Itself, and Inherent (or Unqualified) Happiness.

197.

"Da" Is the Self-Existing Spiritual, Transcendental, and Divine Truth and Reality.

198.

All My Devotees Are Called (and Blessed) To Directly (and Most Directly) Locate "Da" (or Inherently Existing Heart-Bliss) and To Immediately Realize "Da" (or Consciousness Itself) By Means of Most "Radical" or "Perfect" "Hearing" and "Seeing" In My Always Given (and Giving) Company.

199.

The Self-Existing Spiritual Truth and Reality <u>Is</u> "Love-Ananda", Inherent Love-Bliss, or Happiness Itself.

200.

The Self-Existing Transcendental Truth and Reality <u>Is</u> Consciousness Itself, or "Mere" Self-Awareness (Prior To attention and its "objects", "others", or "things").

201.

The Self-Existing Divine Truth <u>Is</u> Existence Itself (the Ultimate Essence of all that arises).

202.

Existence Itself, or Consciousness Itself, <u>Is</u> "Love-Ananda", Love-Bliss, or Happiness Itself.

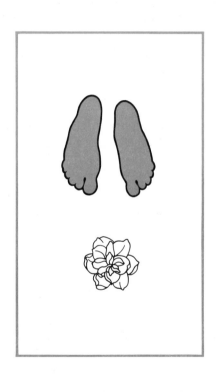

203.

This Is Confirmed By Direct Identification With the Inherent Feeling of Being, or Consciousness Itself.

204.

Therefore, Happiness Need Not Be Sought.

205.

Indeed, Happiness Cannot Be Found.

206.

You Can Only <u>Be</u> Happy.

207.

To Seek Happiness Is To Lose It, Because attention <u>Must</u> Move Out From the Place or Position of Happiness Itself In Order To Seek Happiness Itself.

208.

In every moment of the arising of attention, Inherent Happiness, or Consciousness Itself, or the Native Feeling of Being, apparently <u>Becomes</u> some modification (or objective limitation) of Itself.

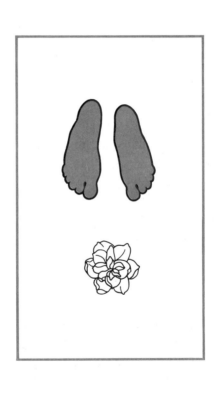

209.

Therefore, in every moment, Transcend the activity (or the apparent tendency) and the apparent effects, or "objects", or "others", or "things" of attention.

210.

Transcend the emotional Motive <u>behind</u> attention.

211.

Transcend the emotional Motive that <u>causes</u> attention to Move Outwardly.

212.

Transcend all the feelings and all the desires that Move (or Motivate) attention.

213.

Transcend every kind of Passionate Attachment to conditional modifications.

214.

Transcend the Entire Event and All the Illusions of attention.

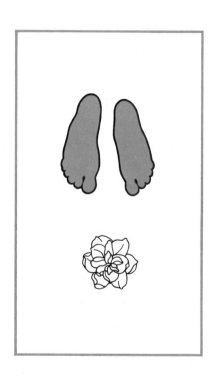

In every moment, Transcend the apparent Loss of Love-Bliss, or of Happiness Itself, by Transcending the Motive, the Motion, the Direction, and the "objects", "others", "things", or relations of attention.

Do This By Directly Re-Locating and Re-Realizing Happiness Itself, in every apparent moment of the arising of attention and all "things".

In every apparent moment of the arising of attention and "things", Re-Locate and Re-Realize Happiness Itself, By Simply Inhering In (or Standing As) Happiness Itself.

Re-Locate and Re-Realize Inherent Happiness (or "Love-Ananda"), and Thereby Re-Locate and Re-Realize Unqualified Self-Awareness, Consciousness Itself, or the Self-Existing and Inherently Free Condition of Spiritual, Transcendental, and Divine Being.

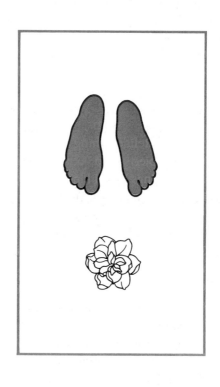

219.

Therefore, Locate the Inherent <u>Feeling</u> (or Constant "Under-Current") of Happiness in every moment.

220.

Locate the Native <u>Feeling</u> (or Constant "Under-Current") of Happiness, and <u>Feel</u> (or Abide <u>As</u>) That.

221.

By (or While) Relinquishing attention to conditional "objects" and "others", "forms" and "states", or "things" of all kinds, Feel Toward Happiness Itself.

222.

The Constant "Under-Current" (or Native Feeling) of Happiness Itself Is Always Already Flowing (or Standing Radiant) In the right side of the Heart.

223.

Even So, <u>If</u> attention is <u>Strategically</u> (or Intentionally) Placed <u>At</u> the right side of the Heart, the Inherent or Native Feeling of Happiness <u>Itself</u> Is <u>Not</u> Found.

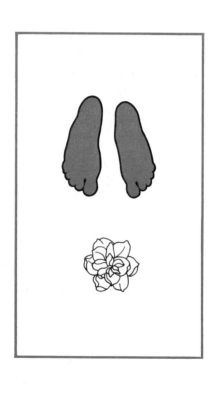

224.

The Inherent Feeling of Happiness Must Be Located Directly, "Merely" by Relinquishing attention to conditional "objects", "others", "forms", "states", or "things", While Feeling Toward Happiness Itself.

225.

If Only Such "Discriminative Feeling" Is Practiced, the Inherent Feeling of Happiness Itself Will Be Naturally (or Spontaneously) Located In (or Via) the right side of the Heart.

226.

All arising conditions (or "things" of attention) are to be "Merely Observed" (or "Witnessed"), Not Sought.

227.

All arising conditions (or "things" of attention) are to be "Merely Observed", as they arise (Spontaneously, or automatically).

228.

All arising conditions (or "things" of attention) are to be "Merely Observed", moment to moment, and in two, or three, or more significantly extended periods of daily Meditation.

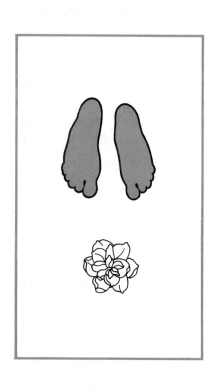

229.

Therefore, Constantly "Witness", "Merely Observe", or Only Feel the self-Contraction and all its "things".

230.

Constantly "Witness", "Merely Observe", or Only Feel "things" (or all "objects", all "others", all "forms", all "states", all relations, the body itself, all sensations, all energies, all perceptions, all emotions, all responses, all reactions, all desires, and all thoughts).

231.

Constantly "Witness", "Merely Observe", or Only Feel all "gross" phenomena, all "subtle" phenomena, all "frontal" (or "descending") phenomena, and all "spinal" (or "ascending") phenomena.

232.

Constantly "Witness", "Merely Observe", or Only Feel all experiences, all "forms" of knowing, All Gestures or Efforts of attention, and the Root-feeling (or "causal knot") of relatedness itself.

233.

Any "thing" and every "thing" that arises should be "Merely Observed", and Thus "Merely" Felt.

234.

Whatever arises (even in the "form" of thought) should be "Considered" In Feeling (and Thus "Compared", In Feeling, to "Perfect" Happiness, and "Discriminated", In Feeling, from Inherent Happiness), without otherwise thinking about what arises.

235.

The "Consideration" (or "Mere Observation") of what arises should be a Feeling-Enquiry (not an exercise of thinking).

236.

"Merely" Feel (and Thus "Merely Observe", or Only "Witness") whatever arises.

237.

Whatever arises, "Merely" Feel it, and Thus Tacitly "Compare" it to "Perfect" Feeling, Inherent Happiness, or Eternal and Unconditional Bliss.

238.

This Is "Radical Understanding": Whatever is "Merely Observed" (or "Merely" Felt) is Soon Tacitly Felt (or Understood) to be mere self-Contraction.

239.

This Is "Real Meditation": Whatever is Tacitly Understood to be mere self-Contraction should be Steadily Ignored, Released, and Forgotten.

240.

This Is "Samadhi",[15] or "Perfect Realization": Whatever is Steadily Ignored, Released, and Forgotten is Directly, "Radically", Inherently, and Ultimately Transcended In the Self-Bliss of Consciousness Itself.

241.

"Merely" to Feel (or "Merely" to Observe) whatever arises, and Thus to Understand, Ignore, Release, and Forget whatever arises, Even to the Degree of "Perfect" Transcendence of whatever arises, Is "Divine Ignorance".[16]

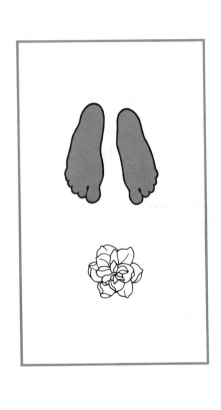

242.

Therefore, whatever arises, "Merely" Feel it, and
Thus "Discriminate" it from Inherent Happiness,
or Uncreated, Unchanging, and Undying Joy of
Being.

243.

Feel Thus.

244.

Is this Happiness?

245.

Is this Happiness?

246.

Is this Happiness?

247.

Feel Thus.

248.

"Compare" Thus.

249.

This is Not Happiness.

250.

This is Not Happiness.

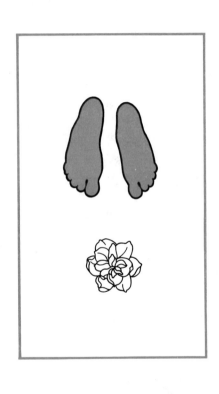

251.

"Discriminate" <u>Thus</u>.

252.

Feel the "<u>Difference</u>" <u>Thus</u>.

253.

In every moment, and By Such "Feeling-Enquiry", the limited and limiting condition that is apparently arising should be Freely Relinquished, or Spontaneously Released, or Easily Felt <u>Through</u>.

254.

Whatever arises Begins to be Ignored, Released, and Forgotten in the very moment of Discovery that the arising condition (or <u>any</u> "thing" of attention) is Not Inherent Happiness, "Perfect" Joy, or Love-Bliss Itself.

255.

Do This "Feeling-Enquiry" moment to moment, and <u>Thus</u> Feel <u>Through</u> whatever arises as a limitation on Feeling, or as an apparent "objective" modification of the "Under-Current" of Happiness Itself.

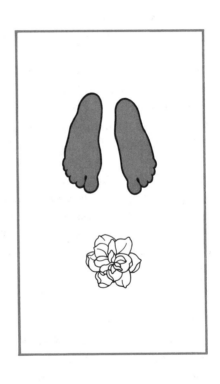

Feel, and Feel Through, and Feel Prior To whatever arises.

By This "Discriminative Consideration" of Feeling, Feel Toward Happiness Itself, Until Prior (or Inherent and Always Already "Perfect") Happiness Itself Is Located.

Happiness Itself Is the Heart, or the "Under-Current", or the Under-Lying Feeling of Being, That Is (apparently) being modified as all conditional "objects", "others", "forms", "states", or "things".

If attention is allowed to move toward its conditional "objects", "others", "forms", "states", or "things", Then Consciousness Itself Feels limited by and to those "objects", "others", "forms", "states", or "things".

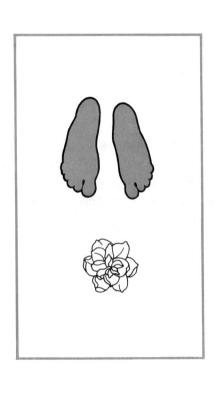

260.

If Consciousness Itself Feels limited to conditional "objects", "others", "forms", "states", or "things", Then Happiness Itself, or the Inherent Feeling of Being, Which Is Consciousness Itself, Seems to be Diminished or Lost.

261.

If attention moves toward "desirable" (or even "undesirable", but "Interesting") "objects", "others", "forms", "states", or "things", Happiness Itself Seems to be Acquired and Attained, So That the Feeling of Happiness Seems to be No Longer Diminished or Lost.

262.

All of That is an Illusion of attention.

263.

All of That is the mind.

264.

All of That is the "Difference" the mind makes.

265.

The mind is the Event and the Illusion of attention.

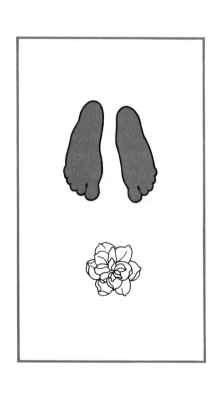

266.

Even "desirable" (or otherwise "Interesting") "objects", "others", "forms", "states", or "things" limit (or Effectively Diminish) Happiness Itself.

267.

The Diminishment (or Loss) of Happiness Itself May <u>Seem</u> Great and Profound in the experience of merely "undesirable" (or Un-"Interesting") "objects", "others", "forms", "states", or "things", whereas, it May Otherwise <u>Seem</u> (<u>Only</u> Because of the Contrast in experience) that Happiness Itself is Greatly and Profoundly Realized in the experience of "desirable" (or "Interesting") "objects", "others", "forms", "states", or "things".

268.

All of That is an Illusion of mind.

269.

All of That is "Difference".

270.

All of That is the Event of attention.

271.

The Event of attention Stands in Clear View, and every Illusion (or "Difference") of mind Is Directly Transcended, By Constant Feeling-Observation and Feeling-Release of <u>all</u> conditional "objects", "others", "forms", and "states" (or all "things").

272.

Therefore, Constantly "Consider" (or "Merely Observe", Feel, "Compare", and Relinquish) whatever is Not Happiness Itself.

273.

Constantly "Re-Cognize" [17] (or know again) and Release whatever is Not Happiness Itself.

274.

In This Manner, Constantly Dissolve (or Feel <u>Through</u>) the arising "things", and Always Toward a <u>Greater</u> Feeling, Until Happiness Itself Is Re-Located In the "Under-Current" of the Heart.

275.

If Happiness Itself Is Located Via Feeling, So That You Naturally and Spontaneously Inhere In, Abide As, and Identify With the "Under-Current" of Happiness Itself In the right side of the Heart, Then Happiness Itself, Which Is the Inherent and Self-Radiant Feeling of Being, Will Be Realized To Be Consciousness Itself.

276.

Happiness Itself, or the Inherent Feeling of Being, or the Self-Radiance of Consciousness Itself, Is Located and Realized Only if attention to conditional "things" is "Merely Observed" and Spontaneously Relinquished In the "Feeling-Enquiry" Toward Happiness Itself.

277.

Therefore, Awaken To This "Radical Understanding" of attention and experience, and Thus Directly Feel, Locate, Inhere In, Abide As, Identify With, and Realize Happiness Itself.

278.

Locate Happiness Itself Thus.

279.

Inhere In Happiness Itself Thus.

280.

Abide As Happiness Itself Thus.

281.

Identify With Happiness Itself Thus.

282.

Realize Happiness Itself Thus.

283.

Stand At, In, and As Happiness Itself,
Relinquishing all else.

284.

Stand As Happiness Itself, Prior To the Urge of
attention toward apparent "things" (or all
apparent modifications and limitations of the
"Heart-Current" of Happiness Itself).

285.

Stand In the Well (or Feeling) of Being,
Naturally and Spontaneously Felt In the right side
of the Heart.

286.

Stand In (and As) the Well of Inherent
Happiness, or Happiness Itself, With No "Other"
Motive.

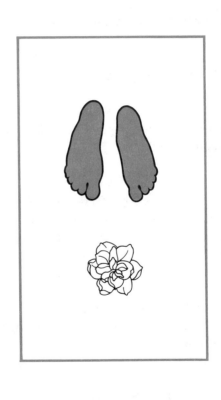

287.

Stand As Consciousness Itself, Self-Radiant As
Love-Bliss, Prior To the body-mind and its
relations or "things".

288.

In any moment, irrespective of what is
apparently arising to attention, Happiness Is
There, At the Origin, the "Subjective" Seat, or the
mindless Transcendental Self of attention.

289.

Therefore, "Feel-Enquire", Feeling Through all
else, Until the Inherent (or Uncaused and
Unthreatened) Feeling of Unqualified, Unlimited,
and Unmodified Happiness Is Located At the
Heart.

290.

Through "Discriminative Feeling", Constantly
Renounce (or Relinquish) attention to "things".

291.

Through "Discriminative Feeling", Constantly
Renounce (or Relinquish) attention to the body-
mind.

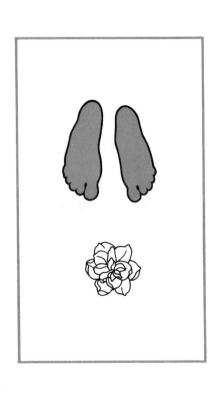

292.

Through "Discriminative Feeling", Constantly Renounce (or Relinquish) the modification, limitation, Diminishment, and Loss of the Inherent Feeling of Happiness, or Love-Bliss Itself.

293.

Through "Discriminative Feeling", Constantly "Feel-Enquire" Toward the <u>Inherent</u> and <u>Un-Diminished</u> Feeling of Happiness (or the Inherent Feeling of Free and Self-Existing Being).

294.

The Inherent and not modified (or objectified) Feeling of Being, Which <u>Is</u> Happiness Itself, <u>Is</u> Always <u>There</u>, Where You "Stand", <u>As</u> You <u>Are</u>, and <u>As</u> the "Under-Current" (or Heart-Feeling) Behind or Beneath or Within or Prior To attention and every "thing".

295.

If You Will "Remember" (or Re-Locate) That "Under-Current" of Feeling (Naturally and Spontaneously Revealed In the right side of the Heart), attention to "things" (or apparent modifications of That Very "Current" of Feeling) Will Relax or Fall or Subside or Resolve In Love-Bliss Itself, or the Inherent Feeling of Being.

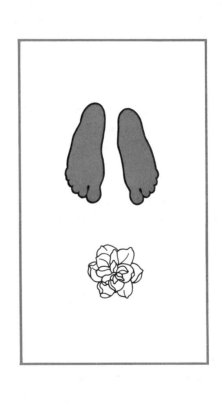

296.

This Re-Location of the "Under-Current" of Heart-Feeling Is the "Perfect" Form of "Conductivity" [18] (or Submission To the "Spirit-Current" of Love-Bliss).

297.

No "Other" (or Additional) Forms of "Conductivity" Are Necessary (or Even Appropriate), <u>When</u> This "Feeling-Enquiry" Is Practiced.

298.

This "Radical" or Most Direct Process of Immediate Realization of the Truth of "things" Is the "Perfect" Form of the "Conscious Process" [19] (or the "Worship" of Consciousness).

299.

No "Other" (or Less Direct) Form of the "Conscious Process" Is Necessary (or Appropriate), <u>If</u> This "Feeling-Enquiry" Is Practiced.

300.

Therefore, Practice "Feeling-Enquiry".

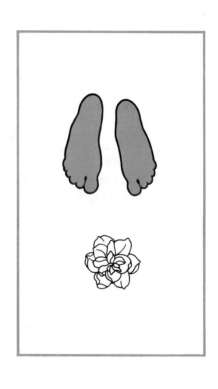

301.

By means of "Feeling-Enquiry", Observe that, Coincident with whatever arises, or whatever "objects", "others", "forms", "states", or "things" Stimulate and Distract attention, <u>There</u> is a corresponding emotion (or emotional sensation).

302.

Therefore, whatever arises, Feel the Coincident feeling (or emotion) associated with it, and "Merely Observe" that it is Not Unqualified and Unlimited Happiness.

303.

By Means of This "Mere Observation", "Remember" the Inherent Freedom and Impulse to Feel Toward (or Re-Locate) the Under-Lying Feeling In Which the present lesser feeling is arising.

304.

In This Manner, Constantly Relinquish lesser feelings, Until the Inherent Feeling (or "Under-Current") of Happiness Itself Is Located.

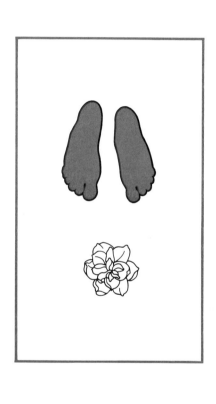

305.

Always "Feel-Enquire" In This Manner, and Thereby Feel the Constant or Native Feeling of Being.

306.

Beneath every kind of lesser feeling (or emotional sensation) that Coincides with attention to "things", There is one Basic lesser feeling that Always arises on the Constant Base of the "Under-Current".

307.

The one Basic lesser feeling that Always Coincides with attention to any "object", "other", "form", "state", or "thing" is the feeling (or emotional sensation) of separation, separateness, and separativeness.

308.

The emotional sensation of separation, separateness, and separativeness that Always Coincides with Every act of attention is the Basic emotional Sign of the self-Contraction.

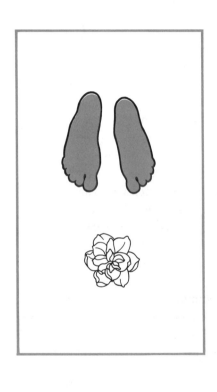

309.

Therefore, mere attention, attention to "things",
or Every act of attention to "objects", "others",
"forms", and "states", is the "Habit of Narcissus",
or the complex avoidance of relationship.

310.

The "Habit of Narcissus", or the complex
avoidance of relationship, is Directly and
Inherently Transcended In (or At) the Heart, or
the "Under-Current" of "Love-Ananda".

311.

Therefore, Constantly Locate and Realize the
Heart of "Love-Ananda".

312.

Constantly "Consider" (or "Merely" Feel,
Relinquish, and Stand Prior To) "Narcissus", the
emotional act and sensation of separation,
separateness, and separativeness.

313.

Always "Feel-Enquire" Toward the Feeling That
Is Always Already Prior To "Narcissus", or the
self-Contraction, and Thus Feel the Constant or
Native Feeling of Being, or Happiness Itself, Prior
To the act and "thing" of attention.

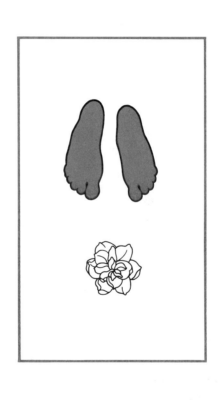

314.

At the Root of attention to any "object", "other", "form", "state", or "thing", Beneath every kind of lesser feeling, and Even Beneath the one Basic lesser feeling that is "Narcissus", or the self-Contraction, There is the "causal" Stress (or Root-feeling and mindless perception) of relatedness.

315.

The Root-feeling of relatedness is the "causal" essence (or Primal Stress) of self-Contraction.

316.

The Root-feeling of relatedness is the Root-"cause" (or Primal conditional essence) of attention itself, all "things", all the emotional Signs of "Narcissus", and all conditional feelings (or all feelings that are less than Happiness Itself).

317.

Paradoxically, the Root-feeling (or "causal" Stress) of relatedness is the Root-essence of self-Contraction, the Root-essence of the avoidance of relationship, and the Root-essence of relationlessness.

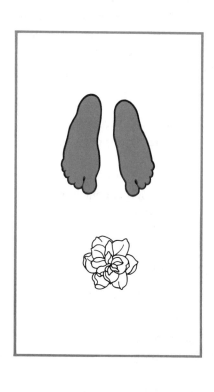

The "causal" <u>Stress</u> (and Root-feeling) of
relatedness is the First Gesture and Very Act of
separation, separateness, and separativeness,
Whereby the Transcendental Divine Condition of
Inherent Happiness is Itself Relinquished.

Therefore, the "causal" <u>Stress</u> (or Root-feeling
and mindless perception) of relatedness is the
principal feeling (or "sensation") to Observe and
Relinquish and Transcend in every moment of
"Feeling-Enquiry".

The Root-feeling and "causal" <u>Stress</u> of
relatedness is Not (itself) "Love-Ananda", or
Happiness Itself.

The Root-feeling and "causal" <u>Stress</u> of
relatedness is merely the First Illusion, and the
First Sign of Bondage to All Illusions.

The Root-feeling and "causal" <u>Stress</u> of
relatedness is the Primal fearful essence of the
act of attention, which Flies From Happiness
(and the Heart).

323.

The Root-feeling and "causal" <u>Stress</u> of relatedness is the Principal Distraction from Inherent Happiness, Because it Leads To all conditional "objects", "others", "forms", and "states", or all "things" (or all that is less than Happiness Itself).

324.

Therefore, Enter Into the Inherent and "Perfect" Feeling of Happiness, Prior To the feeling-<u>Stress</u> of relatedness, Prior To attention, and Prior To any and all conditional "objects", "others", "forms", "states", or "things".

325.

Enter the Domain of the Heart Via the "Spirit-Current" of "Love-Ananda", or the Inherent Feeling of Love-Bliss.

326.

Enter the Domain of the Heart Constantly, Deeply.

327.

Be the "Heart-Current" of Inherent Happiness, Simply.

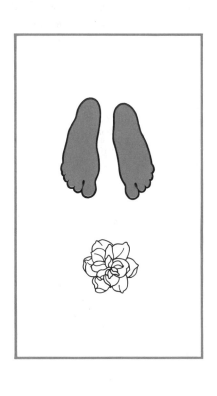

328.

The Under-Lying "Heart-Current" of "Love-Ananda" (<u>By</u> Which and <u>As</u> Which I Bless all beings) <u>Is</u> Happiness Itself, Prior To all limiting modifications.

329.

The Under-Lying "Heart-Current" In the right side <u>Is</u> Self-Radiant and Self-Existing Love-Bliss.

330.

Be Blessed <u>By</u> That, and Abide <u>As</u> That.

331.

Such Is the Natural and Native Means Whereby (and the Very Reality Wherein) all the conditions or "things" of attention (including the Root-feeling and "causal" <u>Stress</u> of relatedness) are <u>Effectively</u> "Turned About", or Relaxed and Resolved In their Transcendental or "Subjective" Source, Which <u>Is</u> Consciousness Itself.

332.

When all conditions of attention Dissolve In the "Heart-Current" of "Love-Ananda", <u>There</u> <u>Is</u> Consciousness Itself.

333.

When Even the Location of the Heart Is Dissolved In Love-Bliss, Consciousness Itself Is the Only Revelation.

334.

The Ultimate Revelation Is Your Very Self.

335.

This Becomes Obvious: Your Very Self Is The Very Self.

336.

Your Very Self Reveals: "I AM", the Only Self.

337.

The Very Self Is One, and Only, but Not separate.

338.

The Very Self Is the One Who Is.

339.

The One Who Is Is God, Truth, or Reality.

340.

The One Who Is Is "Da".

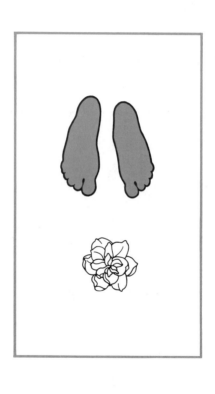

341.

That One "Merely" (or Simply) Is, Always and Already, Prior To the feeling-<u>Stress</u> of relatedness, Prior To attention, and Prior To the feeling of separation, separateness, and separativeness that <u>Always</u> Coincides with attention to any and all "things".

342.

Self-Radiant Happiness, or Consciousness Itself, the Very Heart, <u>Is</u>, Now, Ever-Present.

343.

The Practice of "Feeling-Enquiry" Leads Directly (and Immediately) To This Realization of Consciousness Itself.

344.

Therefore, the Practice of "Feeling-Enquiry" May Appropriately Be Named "<u>The</u> Radical or Most Direct Form of the Way that I Teach".

345.

Even So, the <u>Most</u> "Radical" Practice Is the Practice that <u>Is</u> "Perfect", or <u>Already</u> Awake, or <u>Always</u> <u>Already</u> Established In the Always Already Free Realization of Consciousness Itself.

346.

The Practice of "Feeling-Enquiry" Is a Truly Free (or self-Transcending) Development of the "sixth stage of life".

347.

The Practice of "Feeling-Enquiry" Awakens and Develops Only <u>After</u> (or On the Basis of) True "Hearing" (or self-Observation and self-Understanding).

348.

The Practice of "Feeling-Enquiry" Awakens and Develops Only <u>After</u> (or On the Basis Of) Clear "Seeing" (or Awakening To the "Heart-Current" Through Intuitive "Recognition" of the "True Heart-Master" In God, In Truth, and In Reality, and through Heart-Reception of the Always Already Given and Giving "Blessing" or "Presence" of the "True Heart-Master").

349.

When "Hearing" and "Seeing" Become Suddenly Profound, So That the Search for the "things" of the "first five stages of life" Is No Longer the <u>Motive</u> of Practice, Then "Feeling-Enquiry" May Begin.

181

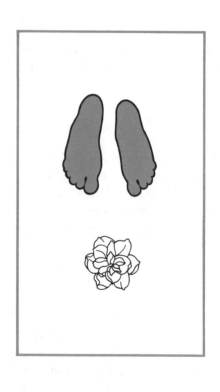

350.

When, Suddenly, Neither the body, Nor the mind (high or low), Nor any of the "things" of the body or the mind is the Motive or the Motivator of Practice, Then "Feeling-Enquiry" May Begin.

351.

When the "Witness-Consciousness" Suddenly Becomes the Obvious Position In Which To View and To Transcend the body, the mind, attention, and all "things", Then "Feeling-Enquiry" May Begin.

352.

The Practice and the Process of "Feeling-Enquiry" Most Directly and Immediately Undermine and Transcend the Outgoing Tendency of attention.

353.

The Practice and the Process of "Feeling-Enquiry" Release and Transcend attention itself, or the complex and Outgoing "Habit" of identification with the body, bodily energies, bodily desires, sensory perceptions, reactive and responsive emotions, and all the "forms" of mind (high and low).

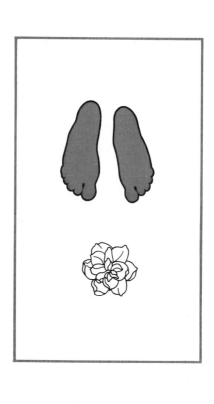

354.

The Practice and the Process of "Feeling-Enquiry" Most Directly and Immediately Transcend all the "forms" of self-Contraction, or egoity, or body-mind, or All Going Out From the Heart of Consciousness Itself.

355.

The Practice and the Process of "Feeling-Enquiry" "Radically" and Most Directly Undermine and Transcend the Practice and the Process of the "first five stages of life".

356.

The Practice and the Process of "Feeling-Enquiry" Immediately (or "Perfectly") Realize That Which Inherently Transcends Even the "sixth stage of life".

357.

The Practice and the Process of "Feeling-Enquiry" Lead Most Directly (and Immediately) To the "Perfect Realization" of Inherent Identification With Consciousness Itself (Prior To all "things").

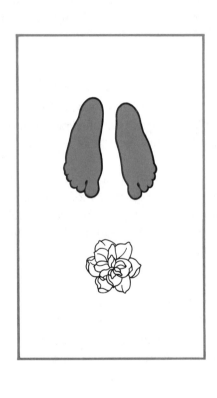

358.

Inherent Identification With Consciousness Itself
Is the Ultimate and "Perfect" Way (or Truly
"Perfect Practice") that I Teach.

359.

Therefore, the "Radical" Practice and the Most
Direct Process of "Feeling-Enquiry" Lead
(Ultimately) To the Great and Incomparable
Realization of Free Enlightenment, "Open
Eyes",[20] "Sahaj Samadhi",[21] or the "seventh stage
of life".

360.

In "Sahaj Samadhi", the One Spiritual and
Transcendental Divine Self Abides Awake, As If
Always With Open Eyes, "Naturally" (or
"Merely") Present As Itself.

361.

When the Eternal Awakeness Is Realized, the
Spiritual and Transcendental Divine Self (or Self-
Radiant and Self-Existing Consciousness Itself)
Spontaneously "Recognizes" all phenomenal
conditions As Transparent (or merely apparent)
and Non-Binding modifications Of Itself.

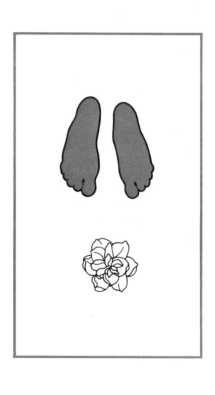

362.

Whatever is Thus "Recognized" is Soon a matter of "Indifference". [22]

363.

Whatever is a matter of "Indifference" is Ultimately "Outshined" In and As the One Spiritual and Transcendental Divine Being and Condition.

364.

When the Totality of Conditional Existence (or all "things", including the body-mind) Is "Outshined" In "Love-Ananda", or the Self-Radiance of Consciousness Itself, That Is "Translation", or Realization of the "Divine Domain". [23]

365.

The "Perfect Practice" of the "seventh stage of life" Is Simply (or Inherently) To Abide As Consciousness Itself (Self-Radiant As Love-Bliss, or Happiness Itself).

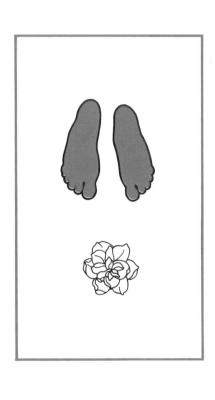

366.

The "Perfect Practice" of the "seventh stage of life" Is To Abide As Consciousness Itself, Inherently and Spontaneously "Recognizing" the body, the mind, attention, and all "things" As Transparent (or merely apparent) and Non-Binding modifications Of Itself.

367.

The "Perfect Practice" of the "seventh stage of life" Is Simply To Be Consciousness Itself, Inherently "Recognizing" all "things" (including the body, the mind, and attention) As Consciousness Itself, and Not "Other" Than Consciousness Itself, or Binding To Consciousness Itself, or Able To Change Consciousness Itself.

368.

The "Perfect Practice" of the "seventh stage of life" Is To Abide As Consciousness Itself, and Thus To "Recognize" (or Ignore, Release, Forget, Inherently Transcend, and Stand Free Of) all conditions that arise.

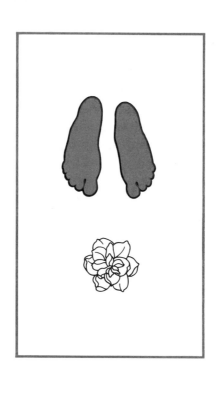

369.

The "Perfect Practice" of the "seventh stage of life" Is Simply To Abide As Consciousness Itself and Thus To "Recognize", Ignore, Release, Forget, Inherently Transcend, and Stand Free Of descent, ascent, all worlds, body, mind, all thoughts, all relations, all "objects", "others", "forms", and "states", all experience, all knowledge, all pains, all the limited and limiting pleasures, fear, sorrow, anger, avoidance, separation, separateness, separativeness, All Seeking, all "things", attention, the Root-feeling and "causal" Stress of relatedness, self-Contraction itself, All Un-Happiness, and Even the Attitude or Presumption of "Witnessing".

370.

The "Perfect Practice" of the "seventh stage of life" Is To Be "Love-Ananda", or Happiness Itself, and Thus To Ignore and Forget death.

371.

The "Perfect Practice" (or "Perfect Process") of the "seventh stage of life" apparently Becomes Progressively "Indifferent" To all that arises, Until all that arises Is "Outshined" By and In and As "Love-Ananda", or Self-Radiant Consciousness Itself.

193

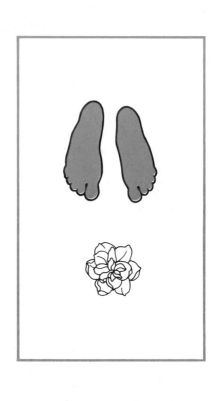

372.

Therefore, "Hear" Me and "See" Me, and Thus "Consider" and Quickly Transcend the Progressive Practice and Process of the Way that I Teach In the Context of the "first five stages of life".

373.

Then "Hear" Me and "See" Me More Directly, or More Happily, and Thus Freely and Surely Embrace the "Radical" or Most Direct Practice of "Feeling-Enquiry".

374.

Then "Hear" Me and "See" Me "Perfectly", Through Profound Submission To the Practice and the Process and the Ultimate Realization of "Feeling-Enquiry".

375.

This "Radical" or Most Direct Practice of "Feeling-Enquiry" Requires True "Hearing", Clear "Seeing", and Exceptional "Dispassion" (or Non-attachment) in the midst of all the Motives and conditions of attention.

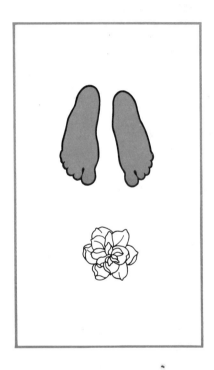

376.

Only True "Hearing", Clear "Seeing", and Exceptional "Dispassion" Allow True, Free, and Ultimately Effective Practice of "Feeling-Enquiry", Because You Cannot Relinquish what You Will Not Cease To Hold.

377.

Therefore, Those Who Embrace This "Radical" or Most Direct Practice of the Way that I Teach Must Be True and Free Renunciates.

378.

I Call All My Devotees to "Hear" Me and to "See" Me, and to "Practice" On the Basis of What They have "Heard" and "Seen".

379.

Do Not Imagine the Call to "Practice" is a Call to merely continue Your ordinary life in body and mind, or Even to Develop an Extraordinary Life in body or mind.

380.

When I Call You to "Hear" Me and to "See" Me and to "Practice", I Mean: Observe, Understand, and Renounce Your ordinary life in body and mind and Your Extraordinary Life in body or mind.

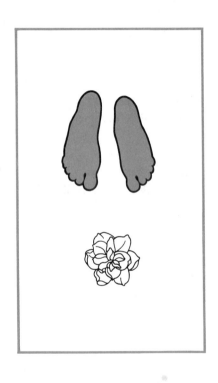

381.

Therefore, Devotees Who "Hear" Me Most Directly and "See" Me Most Immediately also Practice the "Radical" or Most Direct Discipline of Renunciation.

382.

Those Who Practice the "Radical" or Most Direct Discipline of Renunciation Are True and Free Renunciates.

383.

True Renunciates Are True To the One Who Is Truth.

384.

Only They Are True Renunciates Who Are Devoted Exclusively To "Love-Ananda", Inherent Love-Bliss, or Happiness Itself.

385.

Therefore, True Renunciates Renounce whatever is Not Happiness Itself.

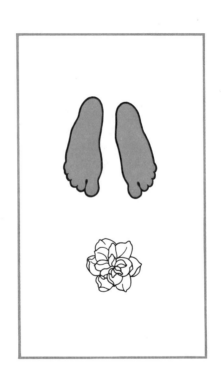

386.

Free Renunciates Stand Free of Passionate Attachment to conditional and apparent relations, or all "objects", "others", "forms", "states", and "things".

387.

Only They _Are_ Free Renunciates Who Have Realized Consistently Free attention.

388.

Only They _Are_ Free Renunciates Who Have Already Disciplined the body-mind, So That it Freely Manifests "Equanimity" (or Constant Purification, Re-Balancing, Regeneration, self-Surrender, and natural Well-being).

389.

Free Renunciates Freely Minimize diet, Limiting food by the "Sattvic Principle" [24] (to what is natural and balanced, pure or non-toxic, whole, fresh, raw, or mostly raw, fruit or vegetable) and, altogether, They Freely (and Always Healthfully) Maintain a "Minimum Optimum" [25] dietary Practice, Strictly Limited to what is Necessary for "Equanimity".

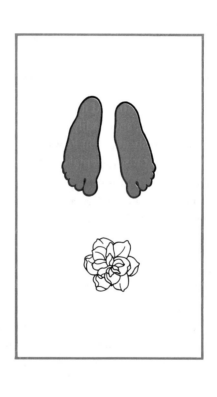

390.

Free Renunciates Freely Demonstrate Radiant
sex-Transcendence (by Releasing sex-Energy and
the sex-function In Motiveless, Purposeless, or
Goal-Free Celibacy), Because sexual activity,
Even in the "Yogic Form" of "Sexual
Communion",[26] is Not Necessary for
"Equanimity", and it Confines and Exhausts the
"Spirit-Current" in the body, and it Fascinates
and Deludes the mind, and it Binds attention to
"objects", "others", and bodily "states", and it
Will Not Relinquish attention itself (to be
Dissolved In its Transcendental or "Subjective"
Source).

391.

Because They Are Always Already Free, All Free
Renunciates Freely Economize, Minimize, and
(Ultimately) Transcend all activities of the body-
mind, or all the activities (and the Very Motive)
of attention itself.

392.

For the Sake of Their Freedom and Happiness, I
Call All My Devotees To (Briefly and Seriously)
Ponder This Most Conservative Practice of True
and Free Renunciation (or "Radical" and Most
Direct Purification, Re-Balancing, Regeneration,
and self-Surrender), and I Call All My Devotees
To the Immediate Practice Of It!   203

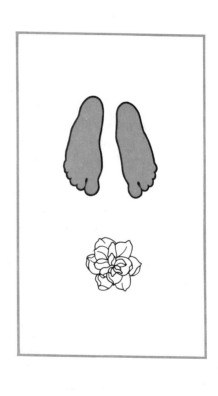

393.

For the Sake of Their Freedom and Happiness, I Call All My Devotees To (Briefly and Seriously) Ponder This "Radical" or Most Direct Practice of the Way that I Teach, and I Call All My Devotees to the Immediate Practice Of It!

394.

When the Essence of "Conductivity" (Which Is True and Free Renunciation of the body-mind) and the Heart of the "Conscious Process" (Which Is the Effective Discipline of attention) Combine To Awaken Native Identification With the "Witness-Consciousness", Then the Great Discipline of the "sixth stage of life" (Free of the "Traditional Error" or Presumption) Spontaneously Begins.

395.

If, On the Basis of True "Hearing", Clear "Seeing", and Real "Practicing" In My Constant Company of Heart-Blessing, the "sixth stage of life" Spontaneously Begins in the midst of the "stages of life" earlier than the "sixth", Then Stand As the "Witness-Consciousness" and Practice "Feeling-Enquiry".

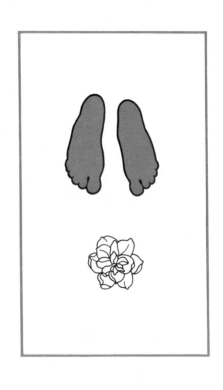

396.

When Native Identification With the "Witness-Consciousness" Awakens, <u>There</u> Is Free or Spontaneous Relinquishment of conditional identification with the body-mind (or the Root-feeling and "causal <u>Stress</u>" of relatedness, which is merely the feeling "I am the body", or "I am the mind", or "I am the body-mind").

397.

The "Witness-Consciousness" Inherently Feels "I Am Consciousness Itself", Rather Than "I am the body", or "I am the mind", or "I am the body-mind".

398.

The "Witness-Consciousness" <u>Only</u> (or "Merely") "<u>Witnesses</u>" (and does not identify with) the body, the mind, or the total body-mind, or the "states" of the body-mind (waking, dreaming, or sleeping).

399.

Therefore, Native Identification With the "Witness-Consciousness" (Rather Than conditional identification with attention and its Motive or its Motions) Is Itself the Confession of Realization and Renunciation.

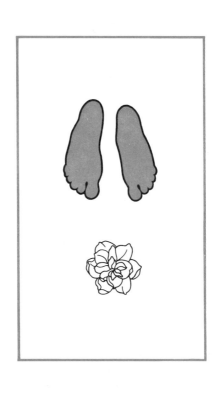

400.

The "Witness-Consciousness" Inherently (At Its Heart) Confesses the Realization "I Am Consciousness Itself".

401.

The "Witness-Consciousness" Inherently Confesses True and Always Already Free Renunciation of the body-mind (and attention to, or via, the body-mind), Because the "Witness-Consciousness" Is Inherently (or Always Already) Free of identification with the body-mind.

402.

Therefore, Native Identification With the "Witness-Consciousness" (Rather Than any effort to avoid, suppress, destroy, or escape the body-mind) Is the Basis or Essence of True and Free Renunciation.

403.

The Native (or Inherent) Confession "I Am Consciousness Itself" Is Also Inherently (and Necessarily) Expressed As the Free (and Identical) Confession "I Am Not the body-mind", or "I Am Not attention", or "I Am, Prior To relatedness and all 'things'".

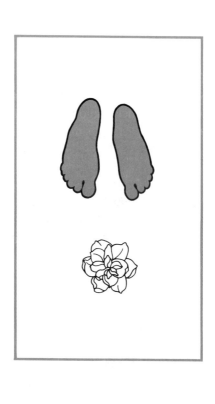

Therefore, Those Who Stand In the Native Position, As the "Witness-Consciousness", Express That Stand Via True and Free Renunciation of All Seeking.

Those Who Stand In the Native Position, As the "Witness-Consciousness", Express That Stand Via True and Free Renunciation of all the Deluding efforts and Binding activities that are the body-mind.

Those Who Stand In the Native Position, As the "Witness-Consciousness", Express That Stand Via True and Free Renunciation of identification with any and all acts and "states" (or results) of attention.

To Stand Most Freely, As the Native "Witness-Consciousness", or As the Free Confession "I Am Consciousness Itself, Prior To the body-mind", Is the Basis of True "Sannyas", or the Great and Awesome Signs of Always Already Free Renunciation of all "things" (Via Total Relinquishment of the Motive of attention itself).

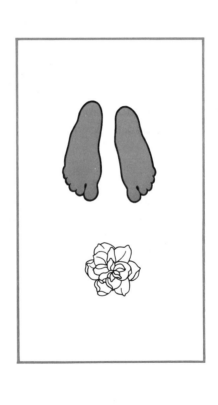

When, In the "sixth stage of life", the Native Confession (and "Perfect Practice") of the "Witness-Consciousness" Is Expressed Via True and Free Renunciation of the body-mind, There Is Inevitable, Soon, and Sudden Realization of the Most "Perfect Practice", or the "seventh stage of life", or "Open Eyes", or Spiritual and Transcendental Divine Self-Abiding (As Consciousness Itself, Self-Radiant and Self-Existing), Even Prior To All "Witnessing", Spontaneously "Recognizing" and Inherently Transcending all the "things" that (apparently) arise In and As "Love-Ananda".

If the "Perfect Practice" of the "seventh stage of life" Is Thus Founded On True and Free Renunciation, Then the Usual Progressive "Transfiguration" and "Transformation"[27] of the body-mind By the Free "Spirit-Current" (In the "seventh stage of life") Becomes Inherently Unnecessary, and Only "Indifference" Increases (apparently, Directly, and Progressively), Until "Translation" (or Sudden "Outshining" of the body-mind and all its "things") In and As "Love-Ananda" (or the Infinite and Eternal Happiness of Consciousness Itself).

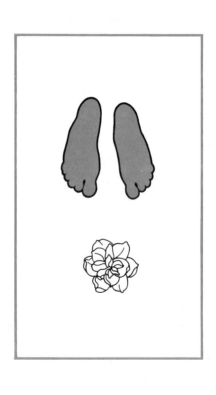

410.

Those Who "Hear" Me and "See" Me "Perfectly" Suddenly Feel the Heart of "things", and the Heart Itself Will "Outshine" the body-mind and all the seeming worlds.

411.

Those Who "Hear" Me and "See" Me "Perfectly" Suddenly Realize the Heart's Inherent Happiness, and They No Longer Seek It Among the "things".

412.

Those Who "Hear" Me and "See" Me "Perfectly" Suddenly Become Heart-True, and Their Renunciation of "things" Is Inevitable, Immediate, Effortless, and Free.

413.

Those Who "Hear" Me and "See" Me "Perfectly" Truly Understand the "Habit of Narcissus", and They Freely Accept My Constant Heart-Blessing Of "Love-Ananda" (That Awakens Consciousness To Itself, "Where" It Is Inherently Free of the body-mind and all its "things").

215

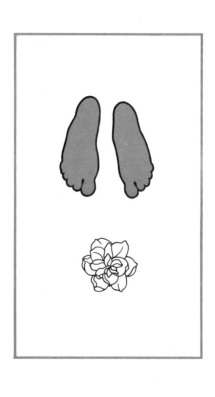

414.

When I Am "Perfectly Heard" and "Perfectly Seen", No "Habit" Will Any More Believe or Make the "thing" of fear, Nor Will Ever the "thing" of attention itself Twist Out of the Heart of Consciousness.

415.

The Who, the What, and the Where That Is Is Only Consciousness Itself!

416.

Only Consciousness Itself Is.

417.

There Is Only Consciousness Itself, and No "Other".

418.

Therefore, Wake Up Sooner Than the mind.

419.

"Merely" Be Who, What, and Where You Always Already Are, Before the "things" of attention arise Therein.

420.

You Are Consciousness Itself (Always Already, and Only).

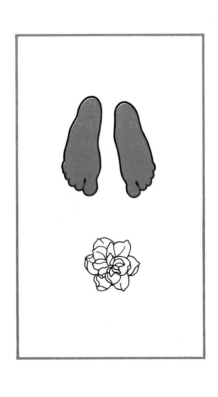

Only Abide <u>As</u> Consciousness Itself, Prior To attention, and "Merely" Self-Aware.

You <u>Are</u>, Inherently Free.

Only <u>Remain</u> Free, Self-Aware, <u>As</u> You <u>Are</u>, Consciousness Itself, and <u>Thus</u> Ignore, Forget, Boundlessly Exceed, and Freely "Fail" To Notice any or every thought (or apparent "thing").

I Have Named the Way that I Teach "Advaitayana Buddhism", the "Radical" (or "Advaitic") Way of One (Not Two), the Inherent (or Eternally Self-Revealed) Way of Transcendental (or Unconditional) Realization of the Who, the What, and the Where of "<u>Is</u>", or the True Renunciate Way of the "Perfect" Transcendence of mind ("buddhi"),[28] or attention itself, In its Always Already Free Source-Condition (Which Is "Bodhi",[29] or Consciousness Itself).

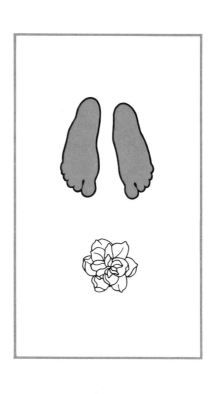

425.

The "Buddhism" of "Advaitayana Buddhism" Progressively (and Then "Perfectly") Magnifies True and Free Renunciation (or Real Transcendence) of the body-mind (and all "objects", "others", "forms", "states", or "things" of attention).

426.

Real (or Effective) Renunciation of the body-mind Is the First Principle (or <u>Effective</u> Sign) of Practice Demonstrated By All Those Who "Hear" Me and "See" Me.

427.

The "Advaitism" of "Advaitayana Buddhism" Progressively (and Then "Perfectly") Magnifies True and Free Renunciation (or Real Transcendence) of attention itself (In its "Subjective", Transcendental, or Non-"objective" Source, Which <u>Is</u> Consciousness Itself).

428.

The Renunciation (or Real Transcendence) of attention In its Transcendental and "Subjective" Source (Coincident With Effective Renunciation, or Real Transcendence, of the body-mind) Is the Second (and Ultimately "Perfect") Principle (or Sign) of Practice Demonstrated By All Those Who "Hear" Me and "See" Me.

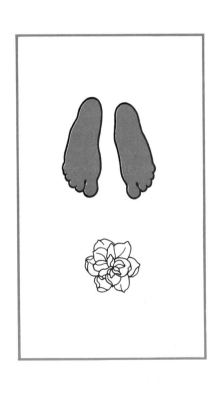

429.

Therefore, Consciousness Itself <u>Is</u> the Ultimate and Most Progressed Discipline, the Most True and Free Renunciation, the Most "Radical" (or Most Direct) Process, and the <u>Most</u> "Perfect Practice" Of The Way that I Teach.

430.

The Way To Realize Consciousness Itself Is Simply To Be (Identify With or Stand <u>As</u>) Consciousness Itself.

431.

You Always Already <u>Are</u> Consciousness Itself.

432.

Therefore, No "Act" of Identification With Consciousness Itself Is Necessary or Fruitful.

433.

"Merely" Affirm (or Effortlessly and Intuitively Presume) Your Always Already Prior and Present Identification With Consciousness Itself By "Merely" Standing <u>As</u> the "Mere Witness" of attention and its "things".

434.

Stand <u>As</u> the "Mere Witness" (or the "Witness-Consciousness") By "Merely Observing" whatever arises.

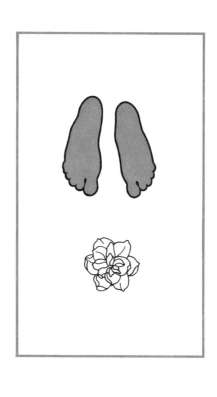

435.

To "Merely Observe" whatever arises Is To Stand Only As the "Witness", irrespective of what arises.

436.

To "Merely Observe", irrespective of what arises, Is to Freely, Only, and Completely (in every detail) Observe the "thing" that is attention itself (or the Root-feeling and "causal" Stress of relatedness) and every "thing" that arises to attention, Without avoiding what arises, or reacting to what arises, or excluding, or desiring, or attaching to what arises, or, in any manner, Seeking (or even following after) any "thing" that arises.

437.

Therefore, "Merely Observe" Exactly whatever "thing" presently arises (as attention itself, or as the "causal" Stress that is the Root-feeling of relatedness, or as the body-mind itself, or as any and every sense-perception, or as any and every "form", "state", "object", or "other", or as any and every "gross" bodily sensation, desire, breath, energy, emotion, or thought, or as any and all the varieties of "subtle" mind, "higher" and mystical vision, waking revery, dream, sleep, and so on), but Do Not avoid or otherwise Seek or follow after any "thing" that arises.

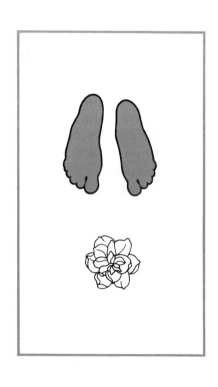

438.

"Merely Observe" avoidance itself, and reactions, and efforts to exclude, and the efforts of desiring and attaching, and Even All the "forms" of Seeking and following after, but Do Not avoid them, or react to them, or exclude them, or desire them, or attach to them, or otherwise Seek or follow after them.

439.

To avoid or, in any manner, to Seek (or even to follow after) "things" Is self-Contraction.

440.

The body-mind, attention, and all "things" are "forms" of self-Contraction.

441.

Likewise, all conditional (or psycho-physical) "Means" (efforts, or Strategies) are themselves (or Inherently) "forms" of self-Contraction.

442.

Therefore, It Is Not Possible to be Free of self-Contraction, avoidance, reaction, exclusion, desire, and attachment (or All the Motions of Seeking and following after "things") By Any "Means" (or any effort of body, mind, or attention).

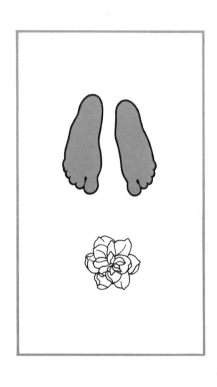

Only the "Witness-Consciousness" Itself Stands Prior To the self-Contraction, "Merely" (or Only) As the Consciousness (or Always Already Free Transcendental and "Subjective" Source) of all that arises.

If whatever arises is "Merely Observed" (or Only "Witnessed"), attention is Immediately Relaxed from Seeking or following after it, and "thing" and attention and relatedness and "causal" Stress and self-Contraction are Progressively (or Even Immediately) Dissolved (or Resolved) In "Love-Ananda", the Native Heart-Feeling of Being, or the Inherent Happiness of Consciousness Itself.

Therefore, to "Merely Observe" "things" (Completely Free of avoidance, reaction, exclusion, desire, and attachment, or All Seeking and following after "things"), it is Only Necessary to Be (or Stand As) the "Witness-Consciousness" Itself.

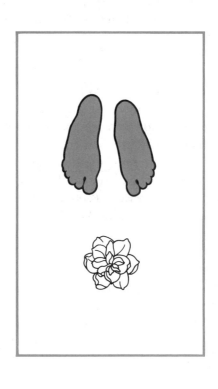

Simply Stand As the "Witness-Consciousness" and "Merely Observe" (Exactly and Completely) whatever presently arises, Until every "thing" (or every "state" of attention) that arises is Immediately Observed, Clearly Felt, and Freely and Tacitly Understood to be Only the experience of self-Contraction (or the feeling of existence, or self, or "I", as a separate and separated "state", or an effort to separate and to be separated and separate).

"Merely Observe" (Exactly and Completely) whatever "things" (or "forms" of self-Contraction) arise, Until It Is Tacitly Observed That Observation Itself (or the "Witness-Consciousness" Itself) Does Not (and Cannot) Seek or follow after any "thing", or otherwise Add self-Contraction, separateness, avoidance, reaction, exclusion, desire, or attachment to Itself (or to whatever "thing" presently arises).

Observe that, irrespective of what arises, You (As "Mere Observer", or As the "Witness-Consciousness") Always Already Stand As Simple Feeling-Awareness.

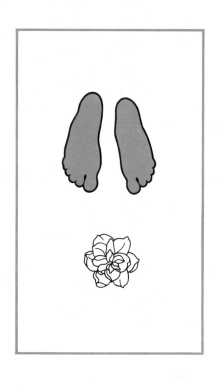

449.

"Merely Observe" self-Contraction itself (or the feeling and effort of separateness), Until it is Tacitly Felt to be Originating (or basically and constantly existing) as the "causal" Stress (or the Root-feeling) of Simple (or mere) relatedness (which Persists Constantly, Even Without, or Prior To, any particular "object", "other", "form", "state", or "thing").

450.

Feel Your "self" feeling (or "Merely Observe" the feeling of relatedness itself, which is itself the Most Primitive essence of the separate "I", and the Original Form of the Illusion of effort), and, In This Manner, Observe and Feel and Directly Realize that attention itself (or the Motion Toward "things") is arising Spontaneously (On its own, as a Mechanical or automatic Event) and Superimposing Itself On the "Witness-Consciousness" (Which Always Remains Constant, Only As Itself, "Merely Witnessing", and Never acting or changing).

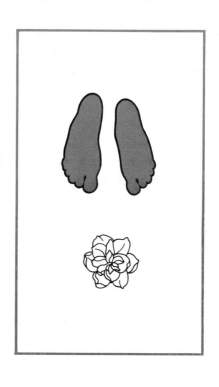

451.

Then "Merely" (and Persistently) Feel (or Be) the Simple (or Motionless) Feeling of Being (the "Under-Current" of "Love-Ananda" That "Merely", Always Already, or Constantly Is), Inherently and Utterly Detached From Involvement With the self-Contraction (or the "causal" Stress and Root-feeling of relatedness, the effort of separateness, the Spontaneous arising of attention, and all Motions, or efforts, Toward "things" of attention).

452.

Do This Entire Cycle of "Mere Observation" and Persistent Feeling (moment to moment, and in Every daily Meditation, and Progressively), Until the "Heart-Current" of Love-Bliss Becomes Obvious and Full In the right side of the chest, and attention (or the Root-feeling and "causal" Stress of relatedness and separateness) is Readily Absorbed (or Collapsed and Dissolved) In It.

453.

Then (As attention Relinquishes all "things" and Subsides In the "Heart-Current") Stand As (or "Merely" Be) the Inherently "objectless" (or Only Self-Existing) Consciousness (or Consciousness Itself) That Was the "Witness" of attention and its "things".

235

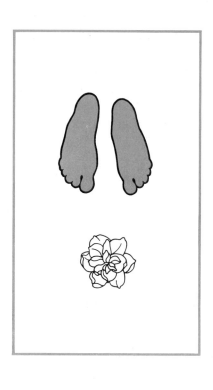

454.

Whatever is "Merely Observed" is Not (and Cannot be) avoided, or reacted to, or excluded, or desired, or attached, or otherwise Sought or followed after, but it is Only "Witnessed".

455.

The "Witness-Consciousness" Is Inherently Non-attached, or Always Already Prior To whatever is "Merely Observed".

456.

Therefore, "Mere Observation" is Not a Method (or Strategy) for Letting Go of self-Contraction (or attention and its "things").

457.

"Mere Observation" (or "Witnessing") Is the Native Position of Consciousness, and Whenever It Is Freely Assumed, There Is (Simply, Spontaneously, and Inherently) No Holding On to self-Contraction (or to attention and its "things").

458.

Therefore, It Is Not Necessary (or Even Possible) To Absolutely Purify the body-mind itself (So That it Becomes "Perfectly" Detached and desireless).

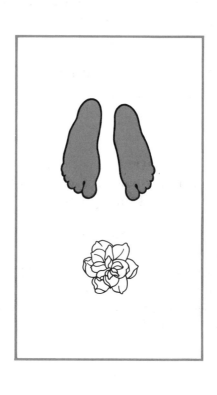

459.

It is Only Necessary (and Always Possible) To Stand As the "Witness-Consciousness" and To Observe (or Realize) That It Is Inherently Pure, Detached, and desireless.

460.

Therefore, Locate and Identify With the "Witness-Consciousness" and "Merely Observe" whatever arises, Until the "Heart-Current" (or the "Mere" Feeling of the "Witness-Consciousness") Begins to Undermine, Absorb, or Dissolve attention itself (or the Root-feeling and "causal" Stress of relatedness), and the total self-Contraction, and All Holding On to "things".

461.

As Holding On Relaxes (or Spontaneously Subsides) In the "Face" of the "Witness-Consciousness", Simply, Freely, and Easefully Allow attention (as the "causal" Stress or Root-feeling of relatedness) to be Dissolved (or Made Indistinguishable) In the "Heart-Current", Until Consciousness Itself (Prior To attention and the "things" of attention) Is Spontaneously Self-Revealed To Be the Native Position, Condition, Content, Being, Self, or "Subject" Who, What, and Where You Are.

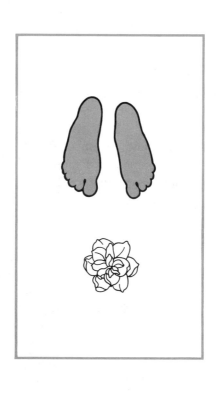

462.

Then Tacitly (and Effortlessly) Abide As
Consciousness Itself, Oblivious to "things".

463.

Soon, whatever arises Will Be Spontaneously
"Recognized" As Only Consciousness Itself.

464.

Then Tacitly (and Effortlessly) Abide As
Consciousness Itself, "Recognizing" all "things",
Even "Indifferent" To all "things", Until the
Inherent Awakeness and Self-Radiance ("Love-
Ananda", or Love-Bliss) Of Consciousness Itself
"Outshines" All Noticing (or all attention to
"things").

465.

Completely Identify With Consciousness Itself,
and Thus Stand Free of All Implication In the
apparent Event of body-mind and world.

466.

Completely Identify With Consciousness Itself,
and Thus Stand Free of all conditional arising, or
All Seeking (and following after), All Contracting
(or separating), All Stimulating and Gesturing of
attention toward "things", or All Needing,
Generating, and Making of Illusions Via the
Event of attention and mind.

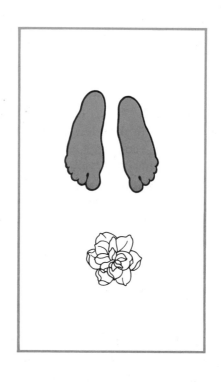

467.

Let This Great Process Develop Progressively, but "Perfectly".

468.

First: In every moment (and in every Meditation), Consciously and Intentionally Stand <u>As</u> the "Witness-Consciousness" and Practice "Feeling-Enquiry".

469.

Second: "Merely Observe" (or "Merely" Feel) every "object", "other", "form", "state", or "thing" (or every process of experience or presumed knowledge) that arises in or as or to the body-mind.

470.

Third: "Merely Observe", but Feel <u>Exactly</u> (or in detail, with all attention to whatever arises).

471.

Fourth: "Merely Observe" (or Freely Feel), Without avoidance, reaction, exclusion, desire, or attachment.

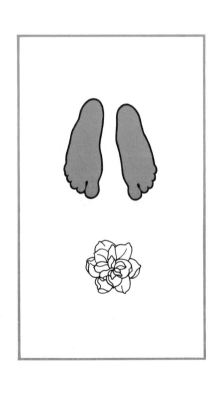

472.

Fifth: "Merely Observe" (or Only Feel), Without Seeking (or even following after) any "object", "other", "form", "state", or "thing" that arises.

473.

Sixth: Constantly "Do" This ("Merely Observing"), or Be Thus (Only "Witnessing"), Until the body-mind (and all experience, and all knowing) is Simply, Clearly, and Directly Felt to be Only self-Contraction (or the effort of separation and separateness).

474.

Seventh: Then Observe and Feel ("Merely" and Directly) that the "Witness-Consciousness" Itself Is Not self-Contraction (but Only the "Witness" of it).

475.

Eighth: Observe and Feel ("Merely" and Directly) that the "Witness-Consciousness" Itself Makes No efforts at all, and It Does Not Create or Add To self-Contraction, and It Does Not Identify With the feeling of separateness.

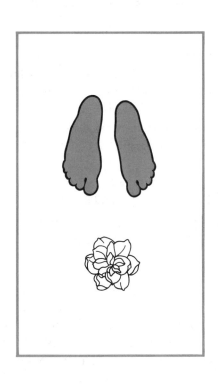

Ninth: "Merely Observe", or Simply Feel, and
Directly Realize that You <u>Are</u> Simple Feeling-
Awareness, "Merely Observing" (or <u>Only</u>
"Witnessing") the self-Contraction in its Original
or Most Primitive "form", which is "causal"
<u>Stress</u>, or the Root-feeling of Simple (or mere)
relatedness.

Tenth: Directly, Simply, and Constantly, "Merely
Observe" the feeling of relatedness itself, Until
You Observe, Feel, and Directly Realize that
attention itself (or the Motion Toward "things")
is arising <u>Spontaneously</u> (On its own) and
Superimposing <u>itself</u> On Simple Feeling-
Awareness.

Eleventh: Persistently Feel and Deeply Identify
With the Constant (or Motionless) "Under-
Current" of "Love-Ananda" (or the Native <u>Feeling</u>
of <u>Being</u>), Which Always Already Stands In the
Feeling-Place, <u>There</u> Where self-Contraction (or
the feeling of relatedness, or attention itself)
arises.

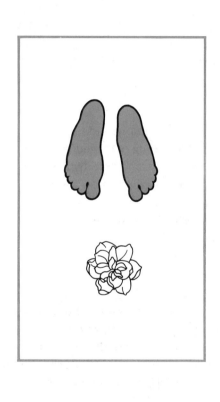

Twelfth: Persistently Feel the Constant "Heart-Current" (In the right side of the chest), Until all "things" are Relinquished and attention itself (or the feeling of relatedness and separateness) Dissolves In "Love-Ananda" (or Boundless Love-Bliss).

Let This Twelve-Part Process of "Feeling-Enquiry" (or "Mere Observation" and Heart-Meditation) Develop Progressively (over time), Step by Step, Until Every Part Of It Is Revealed.

When This Total Process (or Cycle of Twelve Parts) Has Revealed Itself, Repeat It In Its Entirety moment by moment, and in Each Meditation.

When Meditation Becomes Easy Submission To the "Heart-Current", the Exercise of "Mere Observation" of "things" Should (and Will Spontaneously) Be Relaxed and Relinquished.

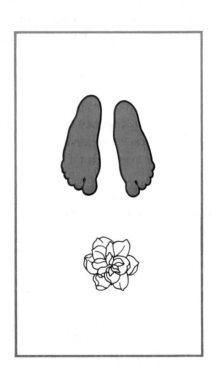

When attention Dissolves (and all "things" are Relinquished) Via the "Heart-Current", You Will Awaken (By Direct Intuition) To the Tacit (and Obvious) Realization that You Are Only Consciousness Itself, Self-Existing (or Self-Radiant) As Love-Bliss.

Then Abide As Consciousness Itself, Oblivious to "things".

When "things" Become "Recognizable", Abide As Consciousness Itself, "Recognizing" all "things".

When "things" Cease to be "Interesting", Abide As Consciousness Itself, "Indifferent" To "things".

When "things" Are Not Noticed, Abide As Consciousness Itself, "Outshining" all "things".

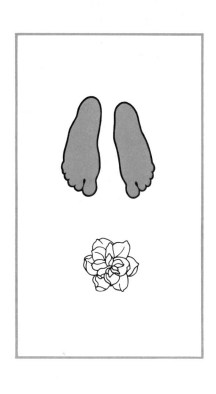

488.

Allow All Of This To Awaken Progressively and To Be Fulfilled "Perfectly".

489.

Therefore, Observe Progressively, but Understand "Perfectly".

490.

Through "Radical" and "Perfect" Understanding, <u>Resume</u> Your Stand <u>As</u> Consciousness Itself, Inherently Free of the Motive Toward "things".

491.

Observe and Understand: All "objects" Evoke need (Anticipating gain).

492.

Need Provokes Seeking.

493.

Seeking Becomes aggressive anger, Failing even <u>before</u> it fails.

494.

And anger is self-inflicted pain.

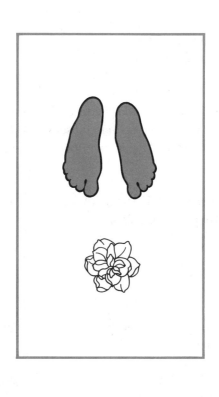

495.

Observe and Understand: All "others" Evoke desire (Anticipating Release).

496.

Desire Provokes attachment and avoidance, Simultaneously.

497.

Attachment and avoidance become sorrow, Inevitably.

498.

And sorrow is the Illusion of emptiness.

499.

Observe and Understand: All "things" Evoke Wonder (How <u>Being</u> Seems a Pair with changes).

500.

Wonder Provokes bewilderment, and also knowledge.

501.

Bewilderment and knowledge Always Contemplate Escape from fear.

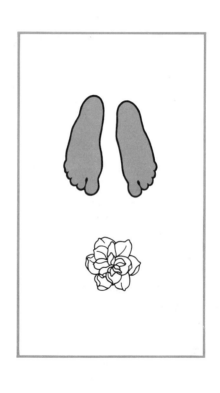

502.

And fear is the Visionary Mood of separateness.

503.

Separateness, emptiness, and pain are the
Constant Complaint, the Un-Breakable "Habit",
and the Inevitable Destiny of the body-mind.

504.

Therefore, whatever arises also Afflicts.

505.

To Understand Is To Stop Resisting This
Understanding.

506.

No "object" is Worthy of need.

507.

No Search is Fruitful.

508.

No pain is Necessary.

509.

No "other" is Worthy of desire and emptiness.

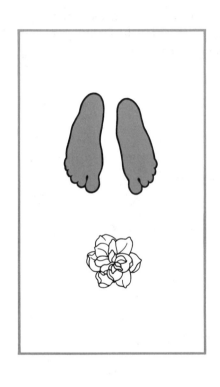

510.

Neither attachment Nor avoidance is Right.

511.

No sorrow is Necessary.

512.

No "thing" is Wonderful.

513.

Neither bewilderment Nor knowledge is Free.

514.

Fear itself is Ultimate pain, but it is Utterly Un-Necessary.

515.

Seeking and attaining are a Total loss, and loss itself is the Only Discovery of gain.

516.

Desiring, even without losing, is emptiness itself, but it is Filled with mind.

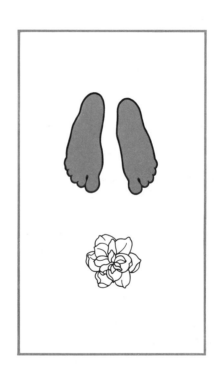

517.

The knowledge of bewilderment (Not "object" or "other") is the only "thing" in mind.

518.

The world of "objects", or "others", or "things", Already bites and Always bites back.

519.

Therefore, Stand Back.

520.

To Seek "objects" (and Not To Understand that All Seeking is Moved by pain) is pain itself, and bewilderment.

521.

To desire "others" or to avoid them (and Not To Understand that desire and avoidance are Made of sorrow) is sorrow itself, and emptiness.

522.

To Wonder and to know "things" (and Not To Understand that knowledge is Never Satisfied) is the Essence of fear itself.

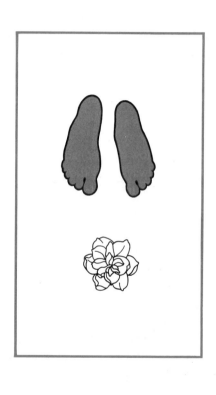

523.

The "personal identity", the ego-"I", or the separate, empty, painful, and self-Contracted body-mind, is Always Already an <u>Illusion</u>, an Un-"Recognized" Reflection of the "Witnessing" Self, a Mirage of need, desirability, and Wonder, Superimposed On Consciousness Itself by the apparent (and <u>Un-Necessary</u>) flow of events that (in themselves) are Not Consciousness.

524.

There <u>is</u> Not (now or Ever) any "personal identity", but <u>Always</u> Only the Ultimate Identity, or Consciousness Itself, Already Free, One, Whole, Full, and All Bliss.

525.

Therefore, Observe and Understand (and <u>Thus</u> Transcend and Forget) the arising Illusion of separation and relatedness.

526.

Be the "Witness" Only, Not separate, Not
related, Not needing, Not Seeking, Not following
after, Not gaining, Not Stressful, Not angry, Not
reacting, Not emoting, Not Full of pain, Not
desiring, Not Fulfilling, Not avoiding, Not
Escaping, Not attached, Not losing, Not sorrowful,
Not lost, Not Wondering, Not thinking, Not
knowing, Not Full of mind, Not perceiving, Not
experiencing, Not Right, Not bewildered, Not
Complaining, Not Wrong, Not fearing, Not
changing, Not Afflicted, Not empty, Not Satisfied,
Not Deluded, Not "attentive", Not Moved, Not
Discovering, Not "I", Not embodied, Not
Released, Not Resisting, Not Even Understanding,
but Only (or "Merely") Being the One Who Is
the "Witness".

527.

Stand There and Be, Consciousness Only,
Inherently "objectless", "relationless", without a
"thing", but Neither separate Nor separated from
All.

528.

Stand Free, and Do Not Look.

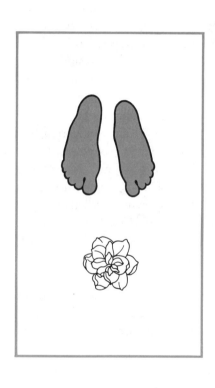

529.

Do Not Indulge attention, Nor Seek the Illusion-mind of "objects", "others", or "things".

530.

Only <u>Be</u>, Bliss-Aware, Consciousness Itself, I Said.

531.

Therefore, I Say, Come To Rest (or <u>Be</u> Awake), <u>Before</u> "things" Happen.

532.

Come To Rest (or <u>Be</u> Awake), <u>Prior</u> To the Motion of separation and relatedness.

533.

Come To Rest (or <u>Be</u> Awake), Already Forever Arrived In My Great Hermitage.

534.

The Heart <u>Is</u> My Hermitage.

535.

My Blessing-Seat <u>Is</u> Consciousness Itself.

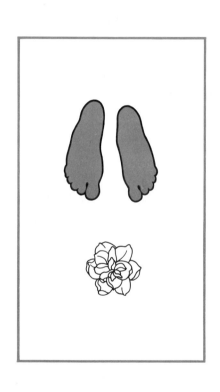

536.

Consciousness Itself <u>Is</u> the "True Heart-Master".

537.

Consciousness Itself <u>Is</u> "Da".

538.

Consciousness Itself <u>Is</u> Self-Existing, Self-Radiant, Inherently Free "Love-Ananda".

539.

I <u>Am</u> Heart-Master Da Love-Ananda.

540.

Consciousness Itself <u>Is</u> the Way that I Teach.

Da Love - Ananda

Notes to the Text of the
Love-Ananda Gita

1. While the popular usage of "radical" indicates an extreme (usually political) position or view, Da Love-Ananda uses the term "Radical" in its original and primary sense, deriving from the Latin "radix" meaning "root", and by extension meaning "irreducible", "fundamental", or "relating to the origin". The "Radical" or irreducible Process directly and immediately penetrates or transcends the ego at its fundamental root or origin, the self-contraction at the heart. (For a discussion of the "causal knot" at the heart, see p. 274, n. 6.)

2. Da Love-Ananda refers to the preparatory practice of the Way that He Teaches as "listening", or giving one's attention to the Teaching Argument and considering it in the context of one's life. In this context, in which Da Love-Ananda is speaking of the most Radical Process of Immediate Realization, a "listener" is anyone practicing in the context of the first five stages of life.

3. Da Love-Ananda has described the psycho-physical and Spiritual development of the human individual in terms of seven stages. The first three stages concern the individual's growth as a functional being on the physical, emotional-sexual, and mental levels successively. The first three stages of life cover personal development from birth to approximately the twenty-first year. Successful adaptation to life at each of these three stages leads to conventional human maturity, when the adult individual is capable of assuming full responsibility for his or her own existence and, most important, for proceeding to explore the higher human possibilities of the remaining four stages of life.

In the fourth stage of life, which represents an important turning point, the individual begins to move fully into the Spiritual dimension beyond the functional and relational concerns that characterize the first three stages. It is in the fourth stage of life that the heart awakens to That which transcends the merely human. The individual becomes capable of heart-felt surrender to and intimacy with the Spirit-Force, the Sacred Reality. At this stage, the individual begins to practice religion in its true sense.

The fifth stage of life is associated with the whole culture of esotericism and mystical spirituality. Here the individual discovers the secret workings of the Spirit-Force within his or her own body-mind. By exploitation of the ascending Current of the Spirit-Power, the fifth stage practitioner can explore all the hidden dimensions of the body-mind and their corresponding cosmic planes. The ultimate attainment of this stage is formless ecstasy ("nirvikalpa samadhi"), which is a temporary immersion into the unqualified Divine Radiance and Consciousness, based on manipulation of the nervous system.

Each of these stages of life is associated with a characteristic error, or sign of egoic seeking. The errors, or neurotic misadaptations, of the first three stages of life are, respectively, the feeling of separation and separativeness (or misadapted individuation), the feeling of being rejected and the need to reject (or misadapted socialization), and the drama of conflict between dependence and independence (or misadapted integration). The fourth stage error is to treat the self as an eternally separate entity and the Divine Being as an Other that is to be sought unendingly. The fifth stage error is to clamor after and cling to all the countless phenomena of mystical introversion, including formless ecstasy. Without true "hearing" in regard to these errors, the experiential phenomena of the first five stages of life are binding and ego-reinforcing distractions that only delay the course of Realization.

The sixth stage represents a major turning point in the Spiritual process. Whereas the first five stages amount to the fulfillment of the experiential possibilities of the body-mind and the world, the sixth stage of life marks the beginning of the primary and direct exercises of self-transcendence and Realization of the Transcendental or Unconditional Reality. From the vantage point of the sixth and seventh stages of life the purpose of the first five stages is to release energy and attention from worldly preoccupation with the functions of the body-mind and to redirect the being from worldly to Spiritual concerns in ever more complete gestures of self-transcendence. Therefore, the first five stages appear as a preparation for the great self-sacrifice called for in the sixth and seventh stages of life.

Da Love-Ananda writes of the sixth and seventh stages:

"In the sixth stage of life, the body-mind is simply relaxed into the Life-Current, and attention (the root or base of the mind) is inverted, away from gross and subtle states and objects of the body-mind, and toward its own Root, the ultimate Root of the ego-self, which is the 'Witness-Consciousness' (when attention is active) and also simple Consciousness (prior to objects and self-definition). The final result of this is conditional Self-Realization, or the intuition of Radiant Transcendental Being via the exclusive self-essence (inverted away from all objects).

"In the seventh stage of life there is native or radical intuitive identification with Radiant Transcendental Being, the Identity of all beings (or subjects) and the Condition of all conditions (or objects).

272

This intuitive identification (or Radical Self-Abiding) is directly Realized, entirely apart from any dissociative act of inversion. And, while so Abiding, if any conditions arise, or if any states of the body-mind arise, they are simply recognized in the Radiant Transcendental Being (as transparent or non-binding modifications of Itself). Such is 'Sahaj Samadhi', and it is inherently free of any apparent implications, limitations, or binding power of phenomenal conditions. If no conditions arise to the notice, there is simply Radiant Transcendental Being. Such is 'Bhava Samadhi', about Which nothing sufficient can be said, and there is not Anyone, Anything, or Anywhere beyond It to be Realized."

While the Way of Realization is characterized by self-transcendence, the first five stages of life in themselves are an ultimately painful and deluding detour into the possibilities of self-fulfillment. Da Love-Ananda's Call has always been to directly Realize the Divine in the seventh stage. With the *Love-Ananda Gita* He reminds us that the whole adventure of self-discovery and other-discovery, particularly in the fourth and fifth stages of life, is unnecessary for one who is truly "hearing" and clearly "seeing".

4. Traditionally, the human body-mind and its environment are seen to consist of three dimensions—gross, subtle, and causal. The gross dimension comprises the physical, etheric (or energy), and lower mental (or the verbal-intentional and lower psychic) aspects of the body-mind. The gross dimension is associated with what Da Love-Ananda calls the "frontal line" of the human body-mind, or the "descended" processes of physical embodiment in the waking state. The subtle dimension, which is senior to and pervades the gross dimension, includes the higher mental (or the higher psychic, mystical, and Spiritual) aspects of the being. And the subtle dimension is associated with the "spinal line" of the body-mind, or the visionary, mystical, and Spiritual processes encountered in dreams, in the internalized or "ascended" experiences of meditation, and after death. The causal dimension is senior to and pervades both the gross and subtle dimensions. The causal dimension is the root of attention, or the essence of the separate self sense. (See also p. 274, n. 6.)

The "Circle" is Da Love-Ananda's term for the circuit of the Life-Current or Spirit-Radiance as It flows through the body-mind. The Circle is composed of two dimensions or arcs, the descending current along the frontal line of the body-mind and the ascending current in the spinal line. In the Radical practice Taught by Da Love-Ananda, the phenomena of both the descending and ascending currents are to be persistently observed, understood, and transcended.

5. Just as each of the first five stages of life is subject to characteristic errors or binding orientations, the sixth stage of life is also characterized by a "Traditional Error". The two aspects of this Traditional Error, as Da Love-Ananda goes on to elaborate them, correspond to the sixth stage limitations on Transcendental Realization associated with the traditions of Buddhism and Advaita Vedanta respectively. For a thorough discriminative treatment of the sixth to seventh stage schools of the Great Tradition and an extended discussion of the correspondences and differences between Advaita Vedanta, Buddhism, and Advaitayana Buddhism, please see *Nirvanasara* by Da Love-Ananda.

6. Prior to God-Realization, each of the gross, subtle, and causal dimensions is expressed in the body-mind as a characteristic "knot". The knot of the gross dimension is associated with the region of the navel. The knot of the subtle dimension is associated with the midbrain, or the "ajna" center directly behind and between the brows. And the knot of the causal dimension, or the "causal knot", is associated with the sinoatrial node (or pacemaker) on the right side of the heart. The causal knot is the primary root of the self-contraction, felt as the locus of the self-sense, the source of the feeling of relatedness itself, or the root of attention.

7. "Recognition" is the Enlightened, or seventh stage, process in which all arising objects, forms, conditions, states, and actions are effortlessly seen as only non-binding modifications of the Transcendental Consciousness that is one's very Self. In *The Dawn Horse Testament,* Da Love-Ananda explains the manner in which the sixth stage error is transcended in the seventh stage process of "Recognition":

> "The Rightly Understood and Rightly Engaged Sixth Stage Practice and Process Will Inevitably (Even If Progressively) Transcend The Sixth Stage Error or Tendency. That Transcendence (or Transcendental Realization) Is In Sahaj Samadhi (or The Free and Truly Transcendental Realization Of Consciousness), In Which conditional objects and states Are Freely Allowed To arise and Even To Be Noticed, and In Which conditional objects and states Are Inherently Recognized As Merely Apparent, Unnecessary, and Non-Binding Modifications Of Consciousness Itself, Which Is Inherently Free As Bliss Itself, Self-Existing and Self-Radiant (and Thus Divine)." (*The Dawn Horse Testament*, pp. 565-66.)

8. In the Teaching of Da Love-Ananda, "Consideration" is the exhaustive reflection upon a particular object, condition, person, pro-

cess, or function until its essential nature is obvious. Consideration in this sense is not merely an intellectual activity, but a process of engaging and submitting one's whole being freely in relationship to the object of consideration. Thus, consideration is a profound Spiritual practice, and, indeed, Da Love-Ananda has at times referred to the entire process of Spiritual life prior to the seventh stage as the "Yoga of Consideration"—the process of testing, considering, and transcending all assumed limits, until Ultimate Awakening in the seventh stage of life.

Da Love-Ananda's use of the phrase "Consideration of Reality" here refers to His great Teaching Considerations whereby He awakened others to the direct feeling-intuition of the Divine Transcendental Reality. By entering into this process of consideration, individuals realize a breakthrough beyond the enclosure of the self-contraction so that what was once perceived as conditional existence may be seen and felt as the Transcendental Divine Reality.

9. Narcissus, the self-lover of Greek mythology, is a key symbol in Da Love-Ananda's criticism of men and women as self-possessed seekers, contracted upon themselves, whose principal and chronic activity Da Love-Ananda summarizes as "the avoidance of relationship".

10. The "Heart" is another name for the Divine Self, the Intuition or Realization of Self-Existing and Self-Radiant Transcendental Divine Being (or God). The origin of the term is the experiential association of Transcendental Self-Realization with the sense of the release of the causal knot felt in the right side of the chest, and the sense of the mind or process of thought and attention falling into its Root or Origin in the "Locus" associated with the trunk of the body.

11. The capitalized "Me" is an Ecstatic expression of the Unqualified Consciousness of the Heart-Master, who has Realized His Identity with the Divine Person, and thus it does not refer exclusively to the individual body-mind.

12. "I AM" is the Ecstatic declaration of the Heart-Master's Realized Identity with Self-Existing and Self-Radiant Transcendental Divine Being. It is Da Love-Ananda's joyful proclamation of the true and eternal Identity of all beings and things, which He says is none other than the Transcendental Self or Blissful Consciousness that mysteriously Stands at the heart of the world and at the heart of Man.

13. The principle of "Remembrance", or Communion with the Divine Person through the Agency and in the Form of the True Heart-Master, is the necessary foundation of the Spiritual process. Throughout His

written Teaching, Da Love-Ananda has pointed to the Guru-devotee relationship as the primary principle of Spiritual practice. It is the "Method of the Siddhas"—the title He gave the first published collection of talks to devotees. And most recently Da Love-Ananda has pointed to this essential principle of the Way as "Ishta-Guru-Bhakti Yoga"—the Way of devotion ("Bhakti Yoga"), or Communion with and ultimate Realization of the Divine Person through the Agency and Person ("Ishta") of the God-Realized Heart-Master ("Guru").

14. Da Love-Ananda has described the area of the heart on the right side of the chest as the center, root, or seat of the Transcendental Self in the body-mind. From the point of view of the body-mind, Consciousness is intuited at a locus that corresponds to the sinoatrial node (or pacemaker) in the right atrium of the heart. However, this area is interpreted as a locus of Consciousness only in the most paradoxical sense, for, strictly speaking, the heart exists in Consciousness, not vice versa. From the "point of view" of Consciousness, there is no "where" other than Consciousness Itself.

15. "Samadhi" is a Sanskrit word meaning literally "placed together". It indicates concentration, equanimity, balance. The term is conventionally used to refer to trance states, spontaneous ecstasies, yogic blisses in meditation, or subtle realizations. Most traditional samadhis are temporary experiences that occur when there is a peculiar intensification of one's energy field. In the present context, "Samadhi" stands for the Blissful Realization of Consciousness Itself, Which stands prior to the movement of attention toward any objects—"Sahaj Samadhi", or the Condition of perfect Enlightenment.

16. "Divine Ignorance" in the Teaching of Da Love-Ananda specifically refers to the intuition of Radiant Consciousness, the Intuitive Realization of which is the fulfillment of the Way. Please see *The Dawn Horse Testament*, chapter 19, for Love-Ananda Da's essential Teaching on Divine Ignorance.

17. "Re-Cognition", which means literally "knowing again", is a technical term in Da Love-Ananda's Teaching. It is the constant non-verbal exercise of Radical insight into bodily and mental activity as contraction, or the dramatization of egoity. In the present context Da Love-Ananda uses the term in a most Radical sense, to indicate the process of insight whereby even the higher discriminative faculty of mind is "known again", or observed, understood, and transcended in Happiness Itself.

18. Da Love-Ananda coined the term "conductivity" to indicate the technical or yogic practice of whole bodily surrender into the All-

Pervading Spirit or Divine Life-Energy. The practice of conductivity is realized through heart-love, or radiant whole-bodily feeling to Infinity. And, as described here, the "Perfect" form of conductivity, which is realized through perfect submission, transcends body and mind in the Inherent Feeling of Being.

19. In the Way of Advaitayana Buddhism Taught by Da Love-Ananda, the "Conscious Process" is a technical term that indicates the senior, Transcendental practice and responsibility of devotees. The "Conscious Process" involves the Radical discipline of the transcendence of attention.

20. In the seventh or Enlightened stage of life the Self no longer seeks to remain concentrated in the heart-root, exclusive of all objects, as in the traditional error of the sixth stage of life. Instead, the "eyes" of the heart open. There is constant and continuous Recognition of all conditions, within and without, as transparent and non-binding modifications of Radiant Transcendental Consciousness.

21. The Hindi term "Sahaj" literally means "together-born", referring to the coincidence of Transcendental Reality with conditional reality. Da Love-Ananda uses "Sahaj Samadhi" as a technical term to describe the fundamental Condition of true, unqualified God-Realization. It is the natural or native Disposition of Identification of the conscious being with the Radiant Transcendental Consciousness, and moment to moment Recognition of all conditions, objects, and states as non-binding modifications of that unqualified Consciousness.

22. Da Love-Ananda has described the process of Transcendental Self-Realization, or the Ultimate Yoga of the seventh stage of life, as a revelation that takes place in four stages—"Transfiguration", "Transformation", "Indifference", and "Translation". If one's movement toward renunciation is strong, the first two stages may be bypassed. Indifference is Inherent Freedom from and lack of concern for all conditional objects, relations, and states. Indifference is discussed fully in chapters 43 and 44 of *The Dawn Horse Testament*.

23. "Outshining" and "Translation" are Da Love-Ananda's terms for the ultimate Event in the Process of Transcendental Self-Realization. If the Yoga of Divine Realization has fulfilled itself within the lifetime of any individual, then at death that individual passes or "Translates" permanently into the "Domain" which is eternally prior to the realms of manifestation.

Da Love-Ananda Ecstatically affirms that there is a "Divine Domain" which is the Destiny of the God-Realized devotee and which transcends space-time and is thus beyond the mind's capacity to comprehend or describe. That Domain is not other than the Heart Itself. Direct Realization of the Divine Domain as the Transcendental Self or Consciousness is the principal import of Da Love-Ananda's Teaching in the *Love-Ananda Gita*.

24. According to Hindu philosophy, all of manifest existence is a play of three qualities, or "gunas". These are inertia (or "tamas"), motion (or "rajas"), and harmony or equilibrium (or "sattva"). Traditionally, "sattva" has been valued above the qualities of "rajas" and "tamas" as the foundation or basis of Spiritual practice. The "Sattvic Principle" in diet is to eat foods that promote balance, harmony, and equilibrium, not overburdening the body, and thus freeing energy and attention for the Spiritual process.

25. For a complete consideration of Da Love-Ananda's Teaching on the "Sattvic Principle" as applied to diet and the process of adapting to and maintaining a "Minimum Optimum dietary practice", please see *Raw Gorilla: The Principles of Regenerative Raw Diet Applied in True Spiritual Practice; The Eating Gorilla Comes in Peace: The Transcendental Principle of Life Applied to Diet and the Regenerative Discipline of True Health;* and the essay "The Illusion of Relatedness" in *The Call to Hermitage*.

26. "Sexual communion" is the technical term used by Da Love-Ananda to describe the natural practice of human emotional and sexual intimacy between lovers wherein body, mind, self-sense, the loved one, and the sexual experience itself are surrendered in direct Communion with the All-Pervading Divine. Da Love-Ananda has always Taught that true practice of sexual communion is not only self-transcending but sex-transcending—that is, it leads beyond and ultimately tends to undermine the motive to sexual activity itself, for precisely the reasons Da Love-Ananda lists here in the *Love-Ananda Gita*.

27. "Transfiguration", generally the first phase of the Enlightened Yoga of the seventh stage of life, is the pervasion of the body-mind by the Radiance of the Divine Light. The process of Transfiguration expresses itself as Blessing in the context of all relations and experiences. "Transformation", generally the second phase of the Enlightened Yoga of the seventh stage of life, spontaneously yields signs and psychic abilities such as the power to heal, longevity, mental genius, and the manifestation of true Wisdom and selfless Love. These processes are discussed more fully in *The Dawn Horse Testament*, chapters 43 and 44.

28. "Buddhi" derives from the Sanskrit verb-root "budh", meaning "to be awake, aware". Traditionally, "buddhi" is the faculty of higher wisdom, or illumined reason, by which one can discern the Real from the unreal. In the process of ultimate Awakening, even this higher discriminative faculty is to be transcended.

29. The Sanskrit word "Bodhi" means literally "Wisdom", or, by extension, "Enlightenment". Thus, the fig tree that is sacred to Buddhists, under which Gautama is said to have been sitting when he attained Enlightenment, is called the "Bodhi tree".

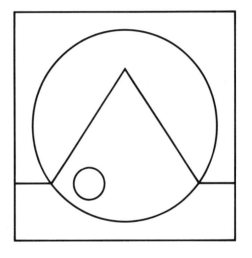

Sacred Logo of The Advaitayana Buddhist Communion

The Principle of Retreat

An Introduction to
The Advaitayana Buddhist Communion

The Communion

The Advaitayana Buddhist Communion is the institutional Agency of the Way that Da Love-Ananda Teaches. Advaitayana Buddhism is not only the "Radical" Wisdom of Da Love-Ananda's own ultimate Realization, but it is the culmination of the Great Tradition, or the total inheritance of authentic religious, Spiritual, magical, and transcendental paths, philosophies, and testimonies from all the eras and cultures of humanity. The name that Da Love-Ananda has given the Communion of His devotees expresses His acknowledgment of the relationship between the Way that He Teaches and the Great Tradition. He explains:

The Way that I Teach is, like the Buddhist Way, realistic, since it is, in its mature form, expressed via free insight into the limiting mechanics of the self rather than via any process of strategic inversion of attention upon the self-essence or of contemplative absorption of the attention of the egoic self in the Divine Spirit or the Transcendental Other. But the Way that I Teach is also, like the Way of Advaita Vedanta, openly oriented toward ultimate transcendence of self and not-self in the Transcendental Reality, Being, Self, or Consciousness. Therefore, the Way that I Teach does not bear an exclusive affinity to either Buddhism or Upanishadic Advaitism (or non-dualism), but it acknowledges both as its most congenial ancient likenesses, and it acknowledges the entire Great Tradition, in all times and places, in all of the stages of life, and in the person of all true Adepts, to be its inherited Tradition.

The Way that I Teach stands on its own merits, and it has arisen freely and spontaneously, without fixed deference to the point of view of any part of the traditions, and without the benefit or the hindrance represented by a significant previous cultural training in the philosophies and practices of the traditions. Even so, the total Great Tradition is the true tradition of all of mankind, and the Way that I Teach is a complete fulfillment of that Tradition as well as a radical point of view that rightly and critically understands and values that Tradition as a whole. Therefore, the Way that I Teach can be called Daist, or Radical Transcendentalism, or the Way of Radical Understanding, or the Way of Divine Ignorance, or the Way of Advaitayana Buddhism.[1]

The primary purpose of The Advaitayana Buddhist Communion, a tax-exempt, non-profit religious organization, is to serve Da Love-Ananda's Work to Awaken individuals directly to the Living Divine Reality. The Communion exists to fulfill four great obligations: (1) to safeguard the Three Sacred Treasures or principal

1. Da Free John [Swami Da Love-Ananda Paramahansa Avadhoota], *Nirvaṇasara* (San Rafael, Calif.: The Dawn Horse Press, 1982), p. 73.

means of Agency, namely, the Heart-Master and the members of the Free Order of Advaitayana Buddhist Renunciates and the Hermitage Service Order, the Noble Teaching, and the Empowered Sanctuaries; (2) to disseminate the Wisdom-Teaching of Da Love-Ananda; (3) to provide cultural and educational services for its members and the general public and to manage appropriate access to the sacred forms of Agency; (4) to give voice in the general public to the Wisdom that counters and balances the modern trends of scientific materialism and religious provincialism.

The Principle of Retreat

Traditionally, when an individual wished to intensify the practice of Spiritual life, he or she entered into a circumstance of retreat, renouncing for a time those activities and habits that might tend to draw energy and attention away from the Spiritual process. Living in a quiet and secluded environment and adopting a simplified mode of living, the individual concentrated all his or her energy and attention on Spiritual practice and the Realization of Consciousness. This "Principle of Retreat" is the foundation of practice in The Advaitayana Buddhist Communion. In the advanced stages and the most Radical expressions of practice, membership in the Communion is characterized by celibacy, a diet of generally raw foods, the Radical practice of "Feeling-Enquiry", and, most important, "Ishta-Guru-Bhakti Yoga", or the Yoga of devotion ("Bhakti") to the Living Divine Person through the personal Agency of the God-Realized Adept (one's

"Ishta-Guru", or the Living Form and Revealer of the Divine Person).

Da Love-Ananda has summarized the foundation of the Way of Advaitayana Buddhism as the two-armed "Principle of Retreat", comprising the supportive "discipline of the body-mind", or renunciation, and the primary "discipline of attention", or understanding. This basic Principle of Retreat, as Da Love-Ananda has pointed out, is the active Principle of the process of Awakening even when one first studies the Teaching or attends a public presentation. At an introductory lecture, for instance, the discipline of the body-mind, or renunciation, is in effect in that one must at least sit in one spot for an hour or two, participating bodily in the occasion of the presentation. The discipline of attention is fulfilled by directing awareness to the consideration at hand. Thus, one forgoes other possible distractions and attractions and devotes oneself, body and mind, to pondering the Teaching Argument.

In the progressive practice of the Way, when one becomes a formal student, the discipline of the body-mind develops via life-conditions (or disciplines in the areas of diet, exercise and health, sexuality, service, etc.), which free energy and attention for the Spiritual process. As one's practice of the Way matures, self-discipline naturally and inevitably becomes full renunciation, or the minimization of all possible distractions from the Spiritual process and the magnification of the disposition of equanimity and self-surrender. The impulse to renunciation is fulfilled in Transcendental Self-Realization, or utter, continuous, and eternal freedom from identification with the body-mind. Following such Realization, renunciation eventually becomes Indifference, or the loss of interest in and the forgetting of conditional existence as, more and more, one is effortlessly absorbed in the Self-Radiant Divine Consciousness.

The discipline of attention, the other arm of the Principle of Retreat, first develops, through study, into real pondering of the Teaching as it applies to the conditions of one's daily life. As one's practice of the Way strengthens, pondering naturally and progressively evolves into the capacity for real meditation. And meditation is ultimately fulfilled in the transcendence of attention altogether, perhaps first in "Jnana Samadhi"[2] (or exclusive Transcendental Self-Realization in the sixth stage of life), but inevitably in "Open Eyes", or "Sahaj Samadhi" (which is continuous Transcendental Divine Self-Realization in the seventh stage of life).

The Radical Form of the Way

Rightly viewed, renunciation is the bodily expression of the Freedom that is awakened in real self-understanding, rather than any form of ascetical seeking. It is not an anxious means to a future goal,

2. "Jnana Samadhi" is the culmination of the sixth stage of life. It is Transcendental Realization of the Divine Self, or Conscious Being, exclusive of all objects and relations. Because it excludes, rather than transcends, the conditional body-mind and its relations, it is a temporary or imperfect Realization, and therefore not to be equated with Enlightenment or God-Realization. As Da Love-Ananda writes in *The Dawn Horse Testament*, "It Is, In Effect, Only Realization Of The Essence Of the conditional or phenomenal self" (p. 590).

but a sign of the present Joy of self-transcending Spiritual practice, or the "sufficiency of Realization". Thus, for those who are most Attracted to this real Happiness, and who have prepared themselves through "hearing" and "seeing", Da Love-Ananda offers the option of Radical renunciation, or a life that minimizes all distractions that might possibly delay the course of Realization.

In addition to this offering of a concentrated practice of renunciation, or the Radical discipline of the body-mind, Da Love-Ananda also offers an intensified form of the process of understanding, or the Radical discipline of attention. Da Love-Ananda describes this practice, which He calls "Feeling-Enquiry", in the *Love-Ananda Gita*. The practice of "Feeling-Enquiry" is founded on the Radical Understanding that cuts immediately through all conditions and experiences to establish the devotee in the "Witness-Position", or the Free Position of Consciousness Itself.

The Radical practices of renunciation and "Feeling-Enquiry" are the core disciplines that lead to rapid fulfillment of the Way. They are Da Love-Ananda's Compassionate creation in order to help devotees bypass or move quickly through stages of experience and knowledge that would ordinarily take many lifetimes.

Thus, practice in The Advaitayana Buddhist Communion, as described in *The Dawn Horse Testament,* may advance progressively (yet still directly) through six stages of study and meditation, renunciate self-discipline, sacramental worship, Spiritual service, and sacred initiation. Or, as described in the *Love-Ananda Gita,* practice may proceed most Radically and directly. Once the foundation principles of true "hearing" and clear "seeing" are established, the devotee may mature swiftly through Radical renunciation and the practice of "Feeling-Enquiry" in the context of the sixth stage of life.

Either form of the Way (progressive and still direct, or Radical and most direct) is an efficacious, auspicious, and most honorable exercise of the Sacred Ordeal of practice. But all should also know that Da Love-Ananda especially invites everyone to consider His Gift-Offering of the Radical or most direct Way. All should contemplate their own capacity to "hear" and to directly renounce and stand Free of self-contraction and all seeking. And all should cultivate the capacity for "seeing", or mature, heart-felt, devotional surrender to and Transcendental Identification with the True Heart-Master.

If, at any stage of progressive practice of the Way, even at the very outset of one's encounter with the Teaching and Blessing-Transmission of Sri Da Love-Ananda, one is authentically moved to embrace the most Radical and direct approach to renunciation and Liberation in this Way, The Advaitayana Buddhist Communion provides forms of practice, education, and testing that fully nurture and develop this great impulse to Transcendental Self-Realization. Fulfillment of the Way can, by Sri Da Love-Ananda's Grace, be swift and miraculously conclusive.

The Sacred Services of
The Advaitayana Buddhist Communion

Three main divisions of the Communion serve its membership and the public:

The Laughing Man Institute is the first of three levels of involvement offered by the Communion. It is the educational body that serves the general public and beginning students by providing presentations, lectures, seminars, and courses intended to serve the serious understanding of Da Love-Ananda's liberating and self-transcending message.

The Advaitayana Buddhist Communion, as well as being the name of the Communion as a whole, is also the name of the body of men and women who freely choose to practice and fulfill the Great Way of the Adept. All of the instructions, initiations, tests, and signs of maturity and realization at each stage of practice have been summarized and described in great detail in the published Teaching of Da Love-Ananda.

The Crazy Wisdom Fellowship is the gathering of devotees who have entered the seventh or Enlightened stage of life. This stage of practice is the real beginning of what Da Love-Ananda calls "the Way that I Teach". The Ultimate Yoga of God-Realization may naturally manifest Enlightened Signs of "Transfiguration" and "Transformation", but it certainly or inevitably demonstrates "Indifference" and, finally, "Translation" (or the

"Outshining" of all arising conditions in Radiant Transcendental Consciousness Itself, the "Divine Domain"). Even in the context of the Yoga of the seventh stage of life, devotees continue in their devotional relationship to Sri Gurudev Da Love-Ananda, recognizing the Divine Person in Him (through His Agency as the Pointer to the Divine Domain and the Revelation of the Divine Domain Itself). This is the stage of practice of the perfectly Enlightened devotee, and this stage of practice is the "Perfect" Realization of the Gift that Da Love-Ananda was born to Give to human beings.

An Invitation

If you would like more information about The Advaitayana Buddhist Communion or active forms of patronage and support, or if you would like to become a participating friend, or if you would like to begin to practice the "Radical" Way of Advaitayana Buddhism Taught by Swami Da Love-Ananda Paramahansa Avadhoota, please write:

The Laughing Man Institute
P.O. Box 12775
San Rafael, CA 94913-2775 U.S.A.

Or write or call any of the Regional Centers listed on the following page.

The Laughing Man Institute
Regional Centers

(This list is current as of spring 1986.)

AUSTRALIA
163 Russell St., 1st floor
Melbourne, Victoria 3001
Australia
03-663-5305

THE NETHERLANDS
Prinsengracht 719
1017JW Amsterdam,
The Netherlands
020-277-600

NEW ZEALAND
21 High Street
CPO Box 3185
Auckland 1, New Zealand
09-390032

UNITED KINGDOM
28 Poland Street
London, W1V 3DB,
England
01-734-4217

NORTHEAST U.S.A.
P. O. Box 6
Auburndale, MA 02166
(617) 965-9711

NORTHWEST U.S.A.
918 N. E. 64th Street
Seattle, WA 98115
(206) 527-0260

NORTHERN CALIFORNIA
740 Adrian Way
San Rafael, CA 94903
(415) 492-0930

SOUTHERN CALIFORNIA
616 Santa Monica Blvd.,
Suite 218
Santa Monica, CA 90401
(213) 393-1953

The Written Teaching of
Swami Da Love-Ananda Paramahansa Avadhoota
(Heart-Master Da Free John)

THE SOURCE LITERATURE

These Source Books present Da Love-Ananda's primary Teaching on the Attributes, Secrets, and Realization of the Heart or Radiant Transcendental Consciousness. They are the epitome of His Teaching.

LOVE-ANANDA GITA (THE FREE-SONG OF
LOVE-BLISS)
*The "Perfect Summary" of "Radical" Advaitayana
Buddhism*
$25.00 cloth

SRI LOVE-ANANDA GITA (THE FREE-SONG OF
LOVE-BLISS)
*The "Perfect Summary" of "Radical" Advaitayana
Buddhism*
Deluxe limp-bound
This special deluxe edition of Da Love-Ananda's magnificent *Love-Ananda Gita* is a pocket-sized volume intended for use by advanced practitioners in The Advaitayana Buddhist Communion. It contains devotional recitations that precede and follow the main text.

THE CALL TO HERMITAGE
On the Principle of Retreat and Immediate Realization of the Transcendental Self
$12.95 paper
The Call to Hermitage contains talks and essays from the period immediately preceding Sri Da Love-Ananda's creation of the *Love-Ananda Gita*. Thus, *The Call to Hermitage* serves as an essential companion volume to the *Love-Ananda Gita*.

THE KNEE OF LISTENING
The Early Life and Radical Spiritual Teaching of Da Free John [Swami Da Love-Ananda]
$8.95 paper

THE METHOD OF THE SIDDHAS
Talks with Franklin Jones [Swami Da Love-Ananda] on the Spiritual Technique of the Saviors of Mankind
$9.95 paper

THE DAWN HORSE TESTAMENT
Of Heart-Master Da Free John [Heart-Master Da Love-Ananda]
$45.00 cloth, $17.95 paper

THE PRACTICAL TEXTS

The following practical texts elaborate the basic life-disciplines that are the foundation of the "discipline of the body-mind" in the Way Taught by Da Love-Ananda.

RAW GORILLA
The Principles of Regenerative Raw Diet Applied in
True Spiritual Practice
$3.95 paper

THE EATING GORILLA COMES IN PEACE
The Transcendental Principle of Life Applied to Diet
and the Regenerative Discipline of True Health
$12.95 paper

CONSCIOUS EXERCISE AND THE TRANSCENDENTAL
SUN
The principle of love applied to exercise and the
method of common physical action. A science of whole
body wisdom, or true emotion, intended most
especially for those engaged in religious or spiritual
life.
$8.95 paper

LOVE OF THE TWO-ARMED FORM
The Free and Regenerative Function of Sexuality in
Ordinary Life, and the Transcendence of Sexuality in
True Religious or Spiritual Practice
$12.95 paper

MANUALS OF PRACTICE

The manuals of practice are listed below according to
the stages of practice Taught by Da Love-Ananda. The
Way begins with "listening" to the message of the
Teacher until true "hearing" or understanding of His
Argument awakens. Then "seeing", emotional conver-
sion, or love of the Divine Person and Presence, fol-

lows. On the basis of "hearing" and "seeing", true practice of the Way begins, and may develop rapidly, or even immediately, into readiness to embrace the "Radical" or most direct form of the Way, as revealed in the *Love-Ananda Gita*. The manuals of practice can usefully be studied not only by practitioners but by anyone interested in the Way Taught by Heart-Master Da Love-Ananda.

LISTENING to the Argument of Truth

These books serve the beginning and concentrated practice of studying and pondering Da Love-Ananda's Fundamental Questions and Teaching Arguments relative to Narcissus (or the self-contraction), Radical Understanding (or direct feeling-transcendence of the self-contraction), and Divine Ignorance (or intuition of Radiant Transcendental Consciousness).

THE FOUR FUNDAMENTAL QUESTIONS
Talks and essays about human experience and the actual practice of an Enlightened Way of Life
$2.95 paper

SCIENTIFIC PROOF OF THE EXISTENCE OF GOD WILL SOON BE ANNOUNCED BY THE WHITE HOUSE!
Prophetic Wisdom about the Myths and Idols of mass culture and popular religious cultism, the new priesthood of scientific and political materialism, and the secrets of Enlightenment hidden in the body of Man
$12.95 paper

THE TRANSMISSION OF DOUBT
*Talks and Essays on the Transcendence of Scientific
Materialism through Radical Understanding*
$10.95 paper

HEARING and Understanding the Truth

Da Love-Ananda Teaches that before true practice of
the Way can begin, "hearing" must unlock the heart
and awaken the motive toward self-transcending God-
Realization and the recognition of the Divine Person
and Presence.

THE DREADED GOM-BOO, OR THE IMAGINARY
DISEASE THAT RELIGION SEEKS TO CURE
*A Collection of Essays and Talks on the "Direct"
Process of Enlightenment*
$9.95 paper

THE WAY THAT I TEACH
Talks on the Intuition of Eternal Life
$14.95 cloth

THE BODILY SACRIFICE OF ATTENTION
*Introductory Talks on Radical Understanding and the
Life of Divine Ignorance*
$10.95 paper

SEEING and the Process of Spiritual Baptism

Real practice of the Way is founded on "seeing", or
Spirit-Baptism, which is the process of emotional con-
version to and Communion with the Living Spiritual

Presence of the Divine Person. Seeing is principally initiated and developed through "Ishta-Guru-Bhakti Yoga", or the esoteric process of devotional recognition of and native identification with the Spiritual and Transcendental Divine Self, Which is Revealed in the Company of the "Sat-Guru" or True Heart-Master.

BODILY WORSHIP OF THE LIVING GOD
The Esoteric Practice of Prayer Taught by Da Free John [Swami Da Love-Ananda]
$10.95 paper

COMPULSORY DANCING
Talks and Essays on the spiritual and evolutionary necessity of emotional surrender to the Life-Principle
$3.95 paper

THE FIRE GOSPEL
Essays and Talks on Spiritual Baptism
$8.95 paper

"I" IS THE BODY OF LIFE
Talks and Essays on the Art and Science of Equanimity and the Self-Transcending Process of Radical Understanding
$10.95 paper

PRACTICE and Realization of the Way

The manuals listed below discuss the mature practice of the "discipline of attention" that begins once the foundations of "hearing" and "seeing" are stable. These books, along with the Source Texts, comprise Da

Love-Ananda's published instructions on the practice and fulfillment of "Ishta-Guru-Bhakti Yoga" and its place in both the progressive and the "Radical" forms of practice of the Way that He Teaches.

THE HYMN OF THE MASTER
A Confessional Recitation on the Mystery of the
Spiritual Master based on the principal verses of the
Guru Gita *(freely selected, rendered, and adapted)*
$9.95 paper

THE BODILY LOCATION OF HAPPINESS
On the Incarnation of the Divine Person and the
Transmission of Love-Bliss
$8.95 paper

THE ENLIGHTENMENT OF THE WHOLE BODY
A Rational and New Prophetic Revelation of the Truth
of Religion, Esoteric Spirituality, and the Divine
Destiny of Man
$14.95 paper

THE PARADOX OF INSTRUCTION
An Introduction to the Esoteric Spiritual Teaching of
Bubba Free John [Swami Da Love-Ananda]
$14.95 cloth

NIRVANASARA
Radical Transcendentalism and the Introduction of
Advaitayana Buddhism
$9.95 paper

THE LIBERATOR (ELEUTHERIOS)
$12.95 cloth, $6.95 paper

EASY DEATH
Talks and Essays on the Inherent and Ultimate
Transcendence of Death and Everything Else
$10.95 paper

FOR AND ABOUT CHILDREN

WHAT TO REMEMBER TO BE HAPPY
A Spiritual Way of Life for Your First Fourteen Years
or So
$3.95 paper

I AM HAPPINESS
A Rendering for Children of the Spiritual Adventure of
Master Da Free John [Swami Da Love-Ananda]
Adapted by Daji Bodha [Swami Daji
Ashvamedhananda] and Lynne Closser [Swami Dama
Devadevananda] from *The Knee of Listening*
$8.95 paper

LOOK AT THE SUNLIGHT ON THE WATER
Educating Children for a Life of Self-Transcending
Love and Happiness
$7.95 paper

INSPIRATIONAL AND DEVOTIONAL TEXTS

CRAZY DA MUST SING, INCLINED TO HIS WEAKER SIDE
Confessional Poems of Liberation and Love by the "Western" Adept, Da Free John [Swami Da Love-Ananda]
$6.95 paper

FOREHEAD, BREATH, AND SMILE
An Anthology of Devotional Readings from the Spiritual Teaching of Master Da Free John [Swami Da Love-Ananda]
$20.95 cloth

PERIODICALS

THE LAUGHING MAN magazine (quarterly)
The Alternative to Scientific Materialism and Religious Provincialism
4 issues, $17.95

CRAZY WISDOM magazine
The Monthly Journal of The Advaitayana Buddhist Communion
(Available only to formal friends and students of The Advaitayana Buddhist Communion)
1 year, $48.00

Available at local bookstores and by mail from

THE DAWN HORSE BOOK DEPOT
750 Adrian Way
San Rafael, CA 94903

Please add $1.25 for the first book and $.35 for each additional book. California residents add 6% sales tax.

If you would like our complete list of books and tapes, including our list of traditional Spiritual literature, please send for our catalog.

INDEX

301